GW00983920

FAMILY CHRONICLES:
Maria Edgeworth's *Castle Rackrent*

THE APPRAISAL SERIES
Irish and English Literature in Context
General Editor: Maurice Harmon

APPRAISAL
IRISH AND
ENGLISH LITERATURE
IN CONTEXT
SERIES

The APPRAISAL series presents, in one volume, *the key essays* — critical, interpretive or contextual — dealing with specific works of literature. These essays may be entirely original, being specially commissioned for the series where the editor considers existing material to be inadequate; or may bring together in a re-edited and structured volume, the most important essays for a full, and up-to-date, evaluation of the work; or, the APPRAISAL volume may combine both of these approaches, in order to achieve the best result.

Individual volumes in the APPRAISAL series are researched, edited and introduced by writers whose academic and scholarly expertise on their own subject is already established.

The General Editor for the series is Maurice Harmon of University College, Dublin.

Published in the series:
The Way Back: George Moore's The Untilled Field *and* The Lake
Editor: Robert Welch, University of Leeds

Alive-Alive O! Flann O'Brien's At Swim-Two-Birds
Editor: Rüdiger Imhof, University of Wuppertal

Family Chronicles: Maria Edgeworth's Castle Rackrent
Editor: Cóilín Owens, George Mason University

FAMILY CHRONICLES:
Maria Edgeworth's
Castle Rackrent

Edited by

Cóilín Owens

Wolfhound Press, Dublin
Barnes & Noble Books, Totowa, New Jersey

First published 1987 WOLFHOUND PRESS, 68 Mountjoy Square, Dublin 1.
First published in the USA 1987 by BARNES & NOBLE BOOKS, 81 Adams
Drive, Totowa, N.J. 07512.

British Library Cataloguing in Publication Data
Family chronicles: Maria Edgeworth's Castle Rackrent.
— (Appraisal series, ISSN 0790-0775; 3).
1. Edgeworth, Maria. Castle Rackrent
I. Owens, Cóilín   II. Series
823'.7   PR4644.C3
ISBN 0-905473-97-3 Wolfhound Press

Library of Congress Cataloguing in Publication Data
Family chronicles
    (Appraisal series)
    A collection of critical essays.
    Includes bibliographies
    1. Edgeworth, Maria, 1767-1849. Castle Rackrent.
2. Family in literature. 3. Ireland in literature.
I. Owens, Cóilín. II. Series.
PR4644.C33F35 1987   823'.7   87-11512
ISBN 0-389-20735-7

Cover portrait: Miss Maria Edgeworth, 1822, Joly Collection
(Courtesy National Library, Dublin)
Portrait on page one: Maria Edgeworth drawn by Adam Buck, c.1790
(Courtesy National Library Dublin)
Cover design: Jan de Fouw
Typesetting: Phototype-Set Ltd.
Printed in Great Britain by Billing & Sons Ltd, Worcester.

CONTENTS

ACKNOWLEDGEMENTS

My thanks to the following individuals and institutions for their help with the preparation of this book: Joanne Altieri of the University of Washington; Walton Beacham of Research Publishing Inc.; Gerry H. Brookes of the University of Nebraska; Marilyn Butler of St. Hugh's College, Oxford; Maurice Colgan of the University of Bradford; W. B. Coley of Wesleyan University; John Cronin of Queen's University, Belfast; Thomas Flanagan of the State University of New York at Stonybrook; Elizabeth Harden of Wright State University; Maurice Harmon of University College, Dublin; Dáithí Ó hÓgáin of University College, Dublin; Eileen Kennedy of Kean College; Dean James F. Kilroy of Tulane University; Roger McHugh, University College, Dublin; James Newcomer of Texas Christian University; Appletree Press, Belfast; Barnes & Noble Books; The University of California Press; Columbia University Press; the English Department, Fenwick Library, and the Center for Research and Advanced Studies, George Mason University; Lauinger Library, Georgetown University; Gelman Library, George Washington University; The Library of Congress; The University of Liverpool; Mouton Publishers, The Hague; The National Library of Ireland; Oxford University Press; Southern Illinois University Press; The Editor of *Studies,* Dublin; and The Editor, *SEL,* Rice University, Texas, Texas Christian University Press.

A special word of thanks to the Dean of the Graduate School, George Mason University, for the support of his office.

Do mo bhean chéile, Julianne, an focal deireannach: buíochas agus grá.

PREFACE

I

Castle Rackrent An Hibernian Tale Taken from Facts, and from the Manners of the Irish Squires, before the Year 1782, first appeared anonymously in London and Dublin in 1800. The original reviewers gave general praise to its technical distinction and directed their remarks to the social and political implications of the novel. The *Monthly Review,* observing that it was "written with singular humour and spirit," noted the author's claim that the behaviour of the Rackrents was extinct: "In these Hibernian Memoirs, we have been highly entertained with the exhibition of some admirable pictures, delineated (as we conceive) with perfect accuracy and truth of character; and we apprehend that, from a due contemplation of these portraits, many striking conclusions may be drawn, and applications made, respecting the necessity and probable consequences of an union between the two kingdoms" (May 1800: 90-91). Later that year *The British Critic* concurred: "This is a very pleasant, good-humoured, and successful representation of the eccentricities of our Irish neighbours. The style is very happily hit off; and the parallel to his story, we apprehend, has been too frequently exhibited." The review then went on to a third aspect of the novel which was to become the focus of much subsequent critical discussion: "The character of 'Honest Thady' is remarkably comic, and well delineated; and we are not at all surprised that the publication should, in so very short a time, have passed through two editions" (November 1800: 555). These three aspects of the novel which caught the attention of the earliest reviewers — literary technique, historical and social content, and Thady's characterization — have remained the loci of critical discussions of *Castle Rackrent.*

Castle Rackrent saw three editions in London and Dublin (1800) before appearing with its author's name in the London edition of 1801. Between then and Maria Edgeworth's death, it ran through seven editions and a German translation (1802), including publications in North Carolina (c. 1802), Boston (1814), and Paris (1841). It was also included in two collected editions (1825, 1832-33) reprinted several times during the nineteenth century. It appeared with *The Absentee* in three editions, edited by Henry Morley (1886), A. T. Richie (1895), and Brander Matthews (1910). All of these editions and that by A. N. Jeffares (1953) are superseded by George Watson's (1964).[1] This text has the benefit of corrections in the author's hand in a copy of the first London edition, her expressed intention that the Glossary appear at the end of the novel, and a collation of all previous publications of *Castle Rackrent*.[2] Robert Lee Wolff's edition (Garland: 1979) is a reprint of the original text.

II

Castle Rackrent is a chronicle of the decline and fall of the house of Rackrent (formerly O'Shaughlin). It traces the effects of accumulated absenteeism, alcoholism, litigation, dissipation, avarice, and weakmindedness on four successive masters, leading to the replacement of the Rackrent family by the son of their former retainer. This retainer, Thady Quirk, tells the entire story in a dialect which reveals something of the sentiment and sly humor which coloured the countryman's view of the Anglo-Irish ascendancy.

In the course of his story we hear of four Rackrents: Sir Patrick the entertainer who is killed by drink (two pages); Sir Murtagh the litigant who is killed in a raging argument (five); Sir Kit the absentee high liver who dies in a duel (thirteen); and Sir Condy the weakminded drunkard who acquiesces in the dispersal of his estate (forty-one). So we observe three levels of action in *Castle Rackrent:* the dissolution of an Irish landed family; the takeover of the squireen Jason Quirk; and the portrait of a clever narrator with an uncertain degree of complicity in all of this pathetic debacle.

Castle Rackrent's portrait of Thady Quirk is the most acute delineation of the mental habits and speech patterns of the Irish countryman found to that point in the literature of Anglo-Ireland. Even if primarily directed to an English readership, the novel implies an attitude towards the native Irish narrator that respects his intelligence and humour, takes some pains to record and interpret his values and culture. For these reasons it is primarily a regional novel; yet in retrospect, *Castle Rackrent* has a larger import because it extends both the subject and the technique of Anglo-Irish fiction. In several ways it is a harbinger of the Irish Literary Revival.

Among the qualities which *Castle Rackrent* shares with the literature of that movement are an affinity with oral literature, a stance between two cultural traditions revealing itself through a penchant for ambiguity, and the depiction of the decline of the "Big House." In this last connection, a line of descent can be traced through Somerville and Ross, George Moore, and William Butler Yeats, in turn the progenitors of Lennox Robinson, Elizabeth Bowen, and contemporary writers such as Aidan Higgins and Jennifer Johnston. Elegies for a disappearing social class persist because of a conservative strain in the Irish imagination, or because distinguished examples transcend their anachronistic social and political circumstances by evoking a more profound and widely appreciated sense of spiritual crisis. For discussions of some aspects of *Castle Rackrent* in this context, the reader is referred to the items by T. R. Henn, W. J. McCormack and John Cronin in the list of Additional Criticism.

Usually consigned to a minor role in histories of the English novel, Maria Edgeworth has been compared with Jane Austen as a novelist of manners, and a critic of her own class's irresponsibility. She is censured for the didacticism of most of her works, but praised for her wit and adroit ambiguity in her best — *Castle Rackrent* and *Ormond*. She is also seen as a figure of the late Enlightenment, yet whose regionalism influenced Scott. More recently, she has been credited as an originator of the Victorian novel of childhood.

III

Marilyn Butler, Maria Edgeworth's authoritative biographer, shows that *Castle Rackrent* has two main material sources: the

Edgeworth family chronicles, and the conversations of an employee on their County Longford estate.[3] A selection of these chronicles and account books has been published as *The Black Book of Edgeworthstown*,[4] which Butler describes as "a family saga compounded of debts and prosperous marriages; successive landlords who were selfishly oblivious of their tenants, and yet were strikingly endowed with personal charm, humour, and finally pathos."[5] Elsewhere Butler tells us that "Maria had acquired from her father the practice of collecting curious specimens of Irish speech, and she liked to entertain the family circle by mimicking the brogue and strange opinions of Edgeworth's steward, John Langan," and that *Castle Rackrent* grew out of a friend's suggestion that these can be developed into something more permanent.[6] The Edgeworth papers and John Langan's oral style, would appear, therefore, to complement one another as the respective sources of the substance and form of *Castle Rackrent*.

A perusal of the family chronicles suggests that the relationship is not quite so neat, however. One passage in the handwriting of Maria Edgeworth's grandfather, for example, describes Sir John Edgeworth (1638-1700/1), apparently a model for Sir Kit Rackrent, thus: "The first years of his life were spent in amusement and diversions as usual amongst young people but he had a taste for play (which seemed to be his greatest foible) however he had the pleasure of losing his money amongst the people of the first quality and distinction in Ireland and England to whom he was probably introduced by his father and his wives relatives the judgments obtained by the Duke of Ormond and Earl of Thomond against his father are Evidence that his father lost money to both these noblemen: the affluent fortune which his lady brought him was greatly lessened by this means and by his Expedition to England in his fathers lifetime. He was in other respects a prudent and ingenious man and one of the finest gentlemen and best bred men of his time. ..."[7] A passage in a subsequent MS adds: "Sir John was in his person ... one of the finest Gentlemen of the age ... his Enemies charged him with Jacobitism but it manifestly appears to have been a base unjust charge for even his private letters to his sons shew that he was most sincerely attached to King William and his Government and this not only through principle but out of gratitude to that great Prince for the many lucrative Employments which he had bestowed on him and for the considerable commissions in the Army which 3 of his sons Enjoyed — if the charge against Sir John about the second hand clothes had been true (which I have great reason to doubt of) the condition Sir John was in in the year 1689 the unsettled State and dawning credit of the government just after the Revolution — might have excused him for availing himself in some respects —."[8]

The rhetoric of these extracts indicates that Maria Edgeworth derived something besides plot material from her family chronicle. For in them we can observe elements which enter the rhetorical stance taken by Thady Quirk (minus, to be sure, the idiom derived from his Gaelic background): the expressed need to maintain a record while not being fully committed to the objectivity it implies, and to the latter end the establishment of a discreet narrative code whereby events may be recorded while their unflattering implications can be evaded or humorously euphemized; a pretended unawareness of what is being revealed; a tone which combines defensiveness and cautious criticism; and the reversal device, one of the major motifs of *Castle Rackrent*, where incidents are first rendered with sympathy, and then bared in a flash of cold light.

IV

This collection is designed to make available to the student of the novel and the Irish Revival the best criticism from a variety of perspectives. It includes a dozen selections from published discussions of the work, two original essays, and a selective annotated bibliography.

John Cronin's succinct biographical sketch is complemented by Marilyn Butler's examination of the circumstances and sources of *Castle Rackrent*. Her magisterial biography *Maria Edgeworth: A Literary Biography* presses a scrupulous examination of letters, records and MSS into the service of sound literary judgments. Her discussion of *Castle Rackrent* and Maria Edgeworth's other Irish novels is somewhat weakened, however, by her irritation with critics who are less detached from Maria Edgeworth's assumptions of social and political privilege.

Ernest Baker sketches Maria Edgeworth's intellectual

background, placing her among the novelists of the Enlightenment and unaffected by the Romantic movement, yet somehow in this singular work rising above the rational constraints implied by this company. Complementing this view is the reading of *Castle Rackrent* as an interpretation of the conflict and common cause between a colonial order increasingly unsure of its hegemony and an emerging native middle class. These social and political changes account for the earliest stage of what later became known as the Irish Literary Revival, in the form of works emphasizing the peculiarities or distinctiveness of native character and custom. Thus *Castle Rackrent* can be viewed as a novel which is instrumental in defining English regional fiction — a thesis ably developed by W. B. Coley — or as contributing to a new meaning of the word "Irish" which was neither Gaelic nor English. Thomas Flanagan's exposition of this development sets the standard for much subsequent discussion of *Castle Rackrent*.

The Irish Literary Revival reclaimed for the culture of modern Ireland its near-forgotten lode of Celtic myth, hitherto neglected folktales and folkways, the shreds of the Irish language, and the heroes — native, Scots-Irish and Anglo-Irish — of the various versions of the national cause. *Castle Rackrent* has a particular interest to the student of this phase of modern cultural and political history. In *An Essay on Irish Bulls* Maria Edgeworth joined her father in disclaiming any interest in native culture: "We moreover candidly confess, that we are more interested in the fate of the present race of it's inhabitants, than in the historian of St Patrick, St Facharis, St Cormuc; the renowned Brien Boru [*sic.*]; Tireldach, king of Connaught; M'Murrough, king of Leinster; Diarmod; Righ-Damnha; Labra-Loingseach; Tighermas; Ollamh-Foldha; the M'Giolla-Phadraigs; or even the great William of Ogham; and by this declaration we have no fear of giving offence to any but rusty antiquaries."[9] Some of the conflicts arising from this stance — reformist, utilitarian, rational, colonial, defensive in two directions (towards the peasantry as well as towards English critics of the abuses of landlords in Ireland) — contribute to the complexities of *Castle Rackrent* and subsequent works issuing from the Irish Big House.

Four selections in this work reflect aspects of this issue. Roger McHugh's remarks summarize a position taken by several previous Irish critics, notably Emily Lawless and Stephen Gwynn:

that Maria Edgeworth knew very little of the contemporary "hidden Ireland," and still less of its cultural traditions.[10] Maurice Colgan pursues a similarly adverse line of argument by examining the implications of what *Castle Rackrent* withholds about eighteenth-century Irish political realities. On the other hand, folklorist Dáithí Ó hÓgáin discerns in the novel evidence of original, reliable observation of the beliefs and customs of Irish country life. Similarly, my own contribution derives from the perception that *Castle Rackrent* gives artistic shape to the polemic of *An Essay on Irish Bulls*.

The principal perpetrator of bulls, Thady Quirk, is the signal triumph of *Castle Rackrent*. The development of this endearing, crafty narrator gives the novel its complexity and colour. Since *The British Critic*, successive readers had found Thady to be variously amusing, servile, naive, unreliable, artless, or ingenious. But in 1967 James Newcomer challenged all of these readings, arguing that *Castle Rackrent* offers us a more complex irony: Thady's story reveals an elaborate deception staged to advance his son's interests. This position generated a few specific responses (see bibliography); but Elizabeth Harden's is the most comprehensive, in her analysis of the narrative strategy of *Castle Rackrent*.

This collection concludes with two discussions of questions arising from the technical singularity and relative freedom from didacticism of *Castle Rackrent* among Maria Edgeworth's works. Joanne Altieri's discerning essay examines the relationship of style and moral purpose, while Gerry Brookes, in a well argued essay, refines previous discussions of the moral content of the novel.

The selections in this volume were made from a sizeable body of commentary. For the reader's convenience, an annotated bibliography of selected additional criticism is appended.

V

In preparing this volume, the editor has made all secondary references formally consistent and keyed all textual citations to George Watson's standard edition.

MARIA EDGEWORTH 1768-1849[1]

John Cronin

Maria Edgeworth's date of birth used to be given as 1 January 1767 but she herself seems to have considered 1768 correct and her latest biographer, Marilyn Butler, concurs. There is no doubt about her place of birth, Black Bourton in Oxfordshire. Her father, Richard Lovell Edgeworth, was the second son of an Anglo-Irish landowner. Richard Lovell inherited his father's property in 1770, his elder brother having died in childhood. All those who have written about Maria have inevitably found themselves writing also about her idiosyncratic and interesting father, with whose long career her own is so inextricably woven. To give Richard Lovell the sort of training which would fit him for his duties as a landowner, his father sent him at the age of sixteen in 1760 to Trinity College, Dublin, but he did little there apart from drinking and gambling. In the following year his father despatched him to Oxford, to live at the house of a friend, Paul Elers, and to enrol as an undergraduate at Corpus Christi College. The amorous young Irishman soon became involved with Elers' eldest daughter, Anna Maria, and eloped with her to Scotland in 1763. When the couple returned to Black Bourton the following year, Richard Edgeworth reluctantly accepted the situation and had the couple legally remarried at Black Bourton. In spite of the romantic circumstances of their union, the pair were never very happy together. He found her lacking in the social graces, almost illiterate and given to constant complainings but, before her early death in 1773, she had presented him with five children of whom four survived. Maria was the third in order of birth and the first girl.

It was during the period of this first of his four marriages that Richard Lovell encountered for the first time a group of intelligent and inventive friends with whom he was to remain in touch for many years. Among these was Thomas Day, a fervent disciple of the educational theories of Rousseau, whose engaging eccentricities far surpassed those of Richard Lovell himself. Others were Erasmus Darwin; Josiah Wedgwood, the potter; James Watt, the engineer and James Keir, an industrial chemist. These men were members of a scientific group known as the Lunar Circle and Edgeworth was introduced into this society in 1766. They shared a common interest in the application of science to the problems of industry and Richard Lovell's lively and inventive mind fitted him admirably for membership. He had a consuming interest in machinery of all kinds, in the invention of a working telegraph system, in the building of all roads and canals, the making of carriages and other types of transportation. Many considered him a crank and an oddity but it may have been the very range of his multifarious interests which earned him this reputation. He was, in fact, quick-witted and creative and might have been taken more seriously by his contemporaries if he had narrowed the range of his interests and pursued one of them to an entirely successful conclusion.

Maria's mother died in 1773, giving birth to a daughter, Anna, and Richard Lovell married Honora Sneyd later in the same year. Maria was now about five years old and seems to have spent a rather lonely childhood. She later recalled that her mother "was always crying" and she found her new stepmother rather cold and distant. The child paid her first visit to Ireland in 1773 when her father, with his new bride, was forced to return to his Irish estate by financial pressures. Two years later, the young Maria was sent to school at Derby, to a Mrs Latuffiere who seems to have treated the girl kindly. She was happy at the school and retained pleasant memories of her teachers in later life. In 1777, Richard and Honora moved back to England and the young Maria could then spend her holidays with them at the new home in Northchurch in Hertfordshire. Honora died of tuberculosis in 1780 and Richard Lovell married her sister, Elizabeth Sneyd, later the same year, a course of action which Honora herself had urged upon him before her death. Maria left her school in Derby in 1781 and went briefly to a more fashionable establishment run by a Mrs Devis at Upper Wimpole Street, London.

In the following year, her father made the move which was to decide the future novelist's entire career. In 1782, Richard Lovell decided that the time had come for him to cease being an absentee landlord and he and his new wife, with the children of his earlier marriages, settled at Edgeworthstown, where Maria was to spend the rest of her long and active life. She was now fifteen, old enough to have formed some views about life, young enough to absorb fresh and vivid impressions of her new and strange environment. She was utterly devoted to her father and seems to have given up her life in England quite happily, in the belief that she would come closer to her father by sharing in his work in Ireland. This she did, collaborating with him in many enterprises, including the education of his large and growing family, until his death in 1817, by which time Maria herself was almost fifty. All her biographers, and they have been many, have had to tackle the vexed question of the extent and nature of Richard Lovell Edgeworth's influence on his celebrated daughter and on her works. At one time it was customary to blame him entirely for the strongly didactic element which pervades the great bulk of her published work but this version of their relationship was exposed as an oversimplification by Roger McHugh as long ago as 1938 in a discerning article in *Studies*. It is there pointed out that "the taste of the time and of her father, and the current of ethical, economic and humanitarian thought which the French Revolution set flowing in English literature, had much to say to this, but it is probable that her own experience as a teacher had even more, and that her didacticism continued a matter of choice".[2] Marilyn Butler, in her biography, also opposes the older view of the father as a pernicious influence on the daughter and argues instead that the truth is quite other. She provides much interesting information from letters and other documents to support her contentions.

At any rate, we know that from the time they settled in Ireland, Maria and her father were involved together in all the business of the estate and that she became a sort of permanent secretary to him, riding out with him to visit tenants, being present with him at the settling of disputes, the payment of rents and all the varied business of a prosperous Protestant Ascendancy landlord. This gave her an opportunity to observe his enlightened improvements to his estate and to get to know at first hand the ordinary Irish people who were to form an important part of her literary material. Her earliest writings were of a specifically didactic nature, since they were stories devised for the education of her own brothers and sisters. These were first written down on a slate and were not put on paper until they had been approved by the family itself. Thus, her early efforts at story-telling constitute an example of her enlightened approach to the education of the young and also of her creative humility and willingness to submit her work to the intensely practical criticism of others. In this way she produced *The Parent's Assistant* in 1796 and, in 1798, she collaborated with her father in a work entitled *Practical Education,* thereby bringing to completion an enterprise on which Richard Lovell had first embarked with his beloved Honora some years earlier.

In the same year of 1798, a desperately troubled one for Ireland, Richard Lovell married his fourth wife, Frances Anne Beaufort, who was a year younger than his daughter, Maria. Happily, Maria and her latest stepmother got on very well together from the beginning and the new marriage did not disrupt Maria's close relationship with her father. She usually submitted her work for his approval but, in one celebrated instance, she broke this rule. She wrote her most famous novel, her first one, *Castle Rackrent,* without him and subsequently refused to alter or extend it at his request. It appeared in 1800, the year in which Ireland lost its Protestant Ascendancy Parliament and was joined in the Union with Great Britain. Both Maria and her father firmly believed that Ireland's welfare would be advanced by the Union but, characteristically, he voted against the measure because of his intense disapproval of the corrupt methods employed to bring it about.

One of Maria's best-known novels of manners, *Belinda,* appeared in 1801 and in the following year she accompanied her parents on a trip to England and France, during which she met many of the leading intellectuals of the day. It was on this trip that Maria had her one and only proposal of marriage, from a Swedish gentleman, the Chevalier Edelcrantz. She turned him down because she was reluctant to leave her family and her home for a distant land, but she seems to have gone on thinking seriously about him for some time afterwards. In 1809 she published the first set of her *Tales of Fashionable Life,* which included her second Irish novel, *Ennui.* The second set of these *Tales,* which included *The Absentee,* appeared in 1812. The last of her specifically Irish novels, *Ormond,* appeared at the time of her father's death, in 1817. She was profoundly affected by his passing and by the sundering of their long partnership. She was to survive him by over thirty years, living on into the terrible years of the Great Hunger, during which she worked tirelessly for the relief of her people in the Edgeworthstown area.

Her active literary life lies between the Union and the Famine and she gradually came to feel that she could no longer bear to write about Ireland. The rational optimism which she shared with her father in their early years in Ireland, their liberal and enlightened plans for non-sectarian schools and benevolent improvement of their tenants' lot, all these were swamped by the dark tide of hunger and violence which deluged Ireland at mid-century. After her father's death, she obeyed his request by editing his *Memoirs* in 1820. She paid several visits to England and, in 1823, called on Sir Walter Scott at Edinburgh and later stayed with him at Abbotsford. Scott returned the visit in 1825. In the same year in which the *Memoirs* were published, 1820, she returned to France and travelled also in Switzerland. She was received everywhere with honour and acclaim. Her last novel, *Helen*, was published in 1834. Her last published work was *Orlandino* in 1848, the profits from which went to raise money for the victims of the Famine. She died on 22 May, 1849.

THE SOURCES AND COMPOSITION OF
CASTLE RACKRENT[1]

Marilyn Butler

A habit of construction which surrounded a single didactic point with a large number of details, episodes, and characters from life required rich sources of material. At the beginning of her career as a novelist, Maria Edgeworth's life had been very secluded, and she did not have enough first-hand material for her richly miscellaneous books. Her first two tales, *Castle Rackrent* and *Belinda*, the only major tales for adults before she saw society for herself in Paris and Edinburgh, are more indebted than any she wrote later to the nearest sources, that is her father and family history. In *Castle Rackrent* much of the material used can be traced. This time the core round which the detail was arranged was the character sketch of Thady rather than a didactic theme, but the method of assembling real-life data was to prove very much in character. The real-life origin of Thady M'Quirk — Edgeworth's steward John Langan — is well known, since Maria for once made no secret of it:

The only character drawn from the life in 'Castle Rackrent' is Thady himself, the teller of the story. He was an old steward (not very old, though, at that time; I added to his age, to allow him time for generations of the family[)] — I heard him when first I came to Ireland, and his dialect struck me, and his character, and I became so acquainted with it, that I could think and speak in it without effort: so that when, for mere amusement, without any ideas of publishing, I began to write a family history as Thady would tell it, he seemed to stand beside me and dictate and I wrote as fast as my pen could go, the characters all imaginary.[2]

Her statement that Thady is the only character drawn from life in *Castle Rackrent* is misleading. She meant by this phrase a conscious, systematic attempt to sketch an individual — and odd references to Langan in her letters certainly confirm that down to incidental gestures Thady was a faithful copy. On the first occasion when she imitated him in a letter, Edgeworth's brother-in-law Francis Fox had been at Edgeworthstown trying to raise men for a force of militia. "Mr. Fox I believe got but one Recruit out of John Langan and to all our enquiries for my Uncle[,] John shakes his head, puts up his shoulder, or changes from leg to leg which are all in him sad tokens of distress."[3] Anyone who has read *Castle Rackrent* will recognize Thady's characteristic manner of washing his hands of a difficulty.

But as for her claim that no one else in the novel was taken from life, what about the other most substantial characters, the Rackrents themselves? The first, Sir Patrick, could be any convivial, hunting Irish squire, such as Maria had heard her father describe, or herself read about in the Black Book. His successor, the mean and litigious Sir Murtagh, more specifically resembles her grandfather's uncles, Robert, Henry, and Ambrose, and much of the legal detail in this part of the story is recognizably borrowed from Richard Edgeworth's family history. The third of the line, Sir Kit, is a cheerful insouciant character who might be either of the seventeenth-century John Edgeworths. He also resembles them in going off to England to steal a rich wife. The details of the marriage, however, are taken from an authentic incident in another Irish family. In the novel Sir Kit brings home a wealthy Jewish bride whose intended function is to get him out of his

financial troubles, but she refuses to hand over her jewels; he shuts
her up in her room, and she is not released until his death in a duel
seven years later. This episode appears so incredible that Maria is
obliged to add a footnote giving her source, the imprisonment of
Lady Cathcart by her husband, Col. Hugh Macguire. Elizabeth
Malyn, Lady Cathcart, married Col. Macguire in 1745; but, when
she refused to hand over to him her property and jewels, he
abducted her to his home in Co. Fermanagh, where he kept her
imprisoned until his death in 1764.[4]

It was therefore by making a strict distinction between the
characters of the people involved (which were drawn from
Edgeworth history), and their *actions* (which came from Col.
Macguire and Lady Cathcart), that Maria was able to deny that
Sir Kit and his bride were drawn from life:

> There is a fact mentioned in a note, of Lady Cathcart having
> been shut up by her husband, Mr. McGuire, in a house in this
> neighbourhood [*i.e. near Edgeworthstown*]. So much I knew, but
> the characters are totally different from what I had heard.
> Indeed, the real people had been so long dead, that little was
> known of them. Mr. McGuire had no resemblance, at all events,
> to my Sir Kit; and I knew nothing of Lady Cathcart but that she
> was fond of money, and would not give up her diamonds.[5]

The remaining Rackrent, Sir Condy, the fullest-drawn of the
four, is again not a deliberate representation of an individual in the
sense Maria meant. But he owed a great deal to the Edgeworth
cousin her father had told her about, the young man who frittered
away his fortune had died penniless.[6] While Maria preferred to
deny that the Rackrents had a source, her father seems to have
connected them with this branch of the family. "In reality the
family from whom this picture was chiefly taken has ceased to exist
these forty years."[7] Condy is a complex figure, however, and he
may have traits of Paul Elers, Maria's maternal grandfather,
whose strange indolence had also taken possession of Richard
Lovell Edgeworth's imagination.

The novel has a glossary, a further compendium of facts, for
which it is needless to trace each source. Two notes, however, have
an unusual history. One, on wakes, was written by Edgeworth.
Another, added by Maria to the fifth edition of 1810, illustrates the
stratagems employed by the Irish in their endless lawsuits; it

describes how a piece of turf was secretly buried by night in a neighbour's property, so that a witness could swear that the ground he stood on belonged to his own master. This incident actually occurred during a lawsuit fought between Maria Edgeworth's grandfather and the great-grandfather of a neighbour, a Mr. McConchy.[8] Thus there are a large number of old family sources for the material in *Castle Rackrent*, although these are rare for the later Irish tales. By then, Edgeworth's first-hand experiences, which were very nearly witnessed by Maria, were probably the most important single real-life ingredient. But in both cases, although she had an unusually good vantage-point as her father's assistant, most of her real-life material was not gathered at first hand: it was had from him . . . .

*

Thady M'Quirk, narrator of *Castle Rackrent*, is the most celebrated, extended, and probably the best character sketch Maria Edgeworth ever made. She was able to bring an old man to life as he would have looked, and as Langan did look: Thady scratches his head under his wig, puffs at his pipe, and moves slowly, an old man and a perpetually puzzled one. His wig does double service as a duster; his greatcoat is buttoned round his neck like a cloak, so that the sleeves "are as good as new, though come Holantide next, I've had it these seven years."

But in the last resort what brings Thady to life is Maria's mastery of his idiom and attitudes. "He tells the history of Rackrent family in his vernacular idiom, and in the full confidence that Sir Patrick, Sir Murtagh, Sir Kit, and Sir Condy Rackrent's affairs will be as interesting to all the world as they were to himself."[9] One of the most important points in the first section of the book is this unconscious provincialism, which is meant to strike the English reader as highly absurd. Thady assumes that the whole world lives within a jaunting-car ride of Castle Rackrent. When Sir Patrick dies, for example, he has a fine funeral: "All the gentlemen in the three counties were at it." This is Thady's most distant horizon, while the real focus of his interest is much more local still: "As I have lived so will I die, true and loyal to the family."

The source of comedy is the eccentricity and superficial inconsistency of his comments, which in fact follow logically from his loyalty to the Rackrents. There is for example the fluctuating tone of his remarks about the wife of the third Rackrent he served under, the Jewish bride of Sir Kit. When he first sees her he is startled by her ugliness. She puzzles him by her total ignorance of Ireland, especially the sights and names he has grown up with since boyhood, and he concludes that she must be a little mad. But as she is now Lady Rackrent he feels obliged to defend her: "I took care to put the best foot foremost, and passed her for a Nabob, in the kitchen."[10] He pities her when her husband shuts her in her room, although loyalty to Sir Kit prevents him from saying anything, and the moment that Sir Kit dies in a duel Thady automatically transfers his allegiance to the "Jewish" as lady and head of the house. But as soon as he discovers her desire to leave Castle Rackrent with all possible speed, he loses interest in her, and his sympathies revert to Sir Kit. "Her diamond cross was, they say, at the bottom of it all; and it was a shame for her, being his wife, not to show more duty, and to have given it up when he condescended to ask so often for such a bit of a trifle in his distresses, especially when he all along made it no secret he married for money."[11]

Thady's commentary does not dominate the second, longer section of the book to the same extent. When Sir Condy is driven by his debts out of Castle Rackrent into the lodge at the gate, Thady goes with him, since it is natural for him to prefer his old master to the new owner, his own son Jason Quirk. Thady's declaration for Condy makes him a participant in the action, but a subordinate one; attention from now on is focused on the last of the Rackrents, and the plight he is in when everyone but Thady has deserted him. The pattern of the earlier section is that a mass of material, often from Edgeworth family sources, is used to illuminate Thady's attitudes. The second section tells a much more coherent and in itself interesting story, but it is not primarily about Thady, and apart from suggesting his puzzlement when he has to choose between loyalty to his own family and to the Rackrents, it does not add to what we already know of his character.

There are not two but three distinct stages in the evolution of *Castle Rackrent*. The first is Maria's own description of the genesis of the tale. She wanted a dynasty of landlords, each of whom would possess a vice characteristic of his species, in order to provide a suitable vehicle for Thady. The first part must have been written between the autumn of 1793 and 1796, probably early in that period rather than late. Two years after it was completed, she added Sir Condy's story, presumably because the situation of a dissipated and abandoned figure particularly interested her. Another motive may have been to find a literary vehicle for some of the election scenes she had heard about from her father in January and February 1796.[12] If this was a direct incentive, 1796 would be a plausible date for the second half of the tale.

It is not difficult to imagine why Maria might have wanted to draw a spendthrift landlord more directly than she had treated any of the earlier Rackrents. She had the vivid example of the cousin Edgeworth remembered from his youth, and at times there are also touches of Elers, even Delaval, about Condy. All had fallen from a high or moderately high estate, had squandered their money, been neglected by their friends; and two of them had died bitterly repentant. Edgeworth was fascinated by these three men, whom he must have described vividly to Maria. Even without her father, she could have found a Sir Condy in the last of her dissipated forebears, Protestant Frank, who died deep in debt and a fugitive from his estate.[13]

The last stage in the evolution of the tale is the Glossary. The entire text of *Castle Rackrent*, with its footnotes, was already in print when the family decided that some further explanation for the public was needed.[14] For the printer's convenience the Glossary therefore had to be bound up with the preliminaries of the first edition of 1800, while in later editions it followed in its more natural position at the end of the text. At the end of October 1798 Maria was preparing to send the manuscript to Johnson in London, and the complete book with Glossary was published in January 1800. The date of the Glossary at least can therefore be pinpointed. It was compiled in 1799, probably in the latter half of the year after the family returned from England.

The time of composition is important, because it helps to explain both the existence of the Glossary and the kind of point it tries to make. The Edgeworths had just returned from a tour in which they had renewed intellectual contact with Edgeworth's English friends, and had discussed Ireland's Union with England from the English end. "The commercial and mercantile world in which we have mixed . . . look upon it as madness in the Irish to oppose what they think so advantageous."[15] Suddenly it must have seemed to

the Edgeworths that the onus was on the Irish to prove that the
English were getting a bargain; so that the light entertainment
Maria was about to produce, which presented the Irish as comic
and irresponsible, was anything but timely. Moreover, the book, if
published now as it stood, would make an odd companion piece
with Edgeworth's economic arguments to the Irish House of
Commons and his appeals for a more progressive policy in
education. All this helps to explain the self-conscious intellectuality
and *Englishness* of the Glossary: the Edgeworths were not merely
interpreting Thady to an audience unfamiliar with his type, but
were trying to dissociate themselves from his primitive attitudes.
Some of the notes, especially the first four, are facetious and
patronizing, but most are of serious scholarly and especially
antiquarian interest, reflecting Edgeworth's membership of the
Royal Irish Academy, and probably Beaufort's too. One of the
notes was, as we know, composed by Edgeworth; another, which
from a literary viewpoint contains very interesting matter, must
originally have been supplied by him. When Maria describes a
scene in which two peasants wrangle in front of the "Editor" in his
capacity as Justice of the Peace, it is clearly her father and not
herself who is meant.

The most recent editor of *Castle Rackrent*, considering the
decision to add the Glossary for the benefit of the English reader,
observes that to a modern reader the Edgeworths seem "over-
solicitous".[16] His assumption here is that their motive in supplying
the Glossary was to make sure that the general public would find
its Irish idioms intelligible. Now the Edgeworths had certainly
spent time worrying about this, as the footnotes to the text and the
Preface show. They "had it once in contemplation to translate the
language of Thady into plain English; but Thady's idiom is
incapable of translation, and, besides, the authenticity of his story
would have been more exposed to doubt if it were not told in his
own characteristic manner".[17] As Mr. Watson rightly points out,
the twentieth-century reader finds this fear exaggerated because
he has become accustomed to dialect in fiction, and so had no
difficulty in following Thady's turns of phrase; some of which, like
"let alone" as a conjunction, have become common usage, as the
Edgeworths foresaw they might. Accurate reporting of dialect was
so rare in the eighteenth century that Maria had no reason to take
it for granted that Thady's manner of narration would not prove

an insuperable block. But in spite of these early doubts the Edgeworths had in fact resolved to go ahead with the book as it stood — Irishisms and all — before they were struck with the further doubts that made them add the Glossary. The most cursory inspection of the Glossary shows that it was not meant as a means of overcoming a linguistic or even a cultural barrier. Its function, which became necessary because of the special politicial circumstances of 1799, was to update the book and make it a means of introducing more serious sociological information about Ireland.

The date of publication of this pioneering and soon very celebrated Irish novel — in the very year of Ireland's Union with England — has been taken to be enormously significant in terms of the story's meaning. *"Castle Rackrent* was to be the brilliant requiem of the Protestant Nation, for Maria Edgeworth had seen its history as the life of a family which rose from obscurity, fought bravely, lost meanly, and at last perished in squalor and pride."[18] She had seen nothing of the kind. The Preface is most insistent that the characters in the story are not the same generation as the one on the point of uniting itself with England:

> The Editor hopes his readers will observe, that these are 'tales of other times'; that the manners depicted in the following pages are not those of the present age: the race of the Rackrents has long since been extinct in Ireland, and the drunken Sir Patrick, the litigious Sir Murtagh, the fighting Sir Kit, and the slovenly Sir Condy, are characters which could no more be met with at present in Ireland, than Squire Western or Parson Trulliber in England.[19]

At least one of Maria's later tales, as well as a mass of contemporary evidence, proves that the race of the Rackrents was not extinct in 1800, yet in a perfectly literal sense *Castle Rackrent* does tell "tales of other times". The material is drawn more consistently than in any other Edgeworth tale from the past, particularly from a family history that goes back as far as a hundred and fifty years — which helps to explain why, deplorable though the Rackrents are, they do not shock Maria. Had rackrenting landlords been common in her own day in Co. Longford, her moral indignation would probably have asserted itself; but since most of the landowners lived elsewhere, and few were ever seen at Edgeworthstown, she had no axe to grind on this occasion. A note of personal complaint is heard only once, when the characterization of Thady is held in abeyance for half a page while he pronounces a diatribe against middlemen, and a long footnote in the Edgeworths' own tones is added for good measure.[20] Apart from this Maria is free to exercise her natural bent for character sketching and anecdote. This is both the strength and weakness of *Castle Rackrent*. It does not give away Maria's personal immaturity, as the other early tales do. But if it exposes little, it also expresses little.

In the very nature of its material *Castle Rackrent* is one kind of historical novel, but at a more serious level it is the least historical of Maria's tales. There is no sense of the impending future in it — no clash between the Rackrents' values and those of the people replacing them. *Castle Rackrent* has been read as a forerunner of *Waverley* in its historical awareness. "Sir Condy is a historical as well as a national type; like the Baron Bradwardine in Scott's novel, he is the man who lives by the barbaric standard of honour in a commercial society where that standard can no longer apply."[21] But who in the novel represents the new commercial ethos — is it Jason? Certainly not in the Edgeworths' eyes, because Jason made his fortune as agent to the estate, through the carelessness of the absentee Sir Kit: he was the parasite of the old system, not the herald of a new. It was the very absence in *Castle Rackrent* of a sense of Ireland's economic possibilities that the Edgeworths regretted in 1799; they would not have taken such pains to provide a modern ethos in the Glossary had they felt that it was present in the book.

For reasons which have largely to do with Ireland's later history, the modern reader is likely to sympathize with Thady and to see his attitudes as genuinely rooted in native Irish custom. Because he does so he misses the ironic point that Maria makes very clearly in the first section of the narrative. The Preface states that if it is truth we are concerned with, an illiterate peasant is a more useful narrator than an educated person, because his prejudices and absurdities are too blatant to be mistaken by the reader. With a confidence in objective truth typical of the Enlightenment, the Edgeworths did not allow for a reader who might use historical insight to account for Thady's attitudes. The first half of the book, in which Thady's prejudices, provincialism, and blind partiality for the Rackrents are heavily stressed, only partially gets across to most modern readers. We tend to see all these qualities as typical of a peasant, and therefore as part, a very truthful part, of Maria's impersonation of Thady. She expected us to feel more surprised and more critical, to reject actively his indulgent view of the Rackrents, and supply the correct, the enlightened, moral frame of reference.

This is how Thady's inconsistency and narrowness of vision probably appeared to its first readers. Conceivably it would still have done so if *Castle Rackrent* had been in one part instead of two. The addition of Sir Condy, and Thady's more active part in relation to him, decide the issue against the grain of the first section of the book. It is impossible for a rational person to approve of Sir Murtagh and Sir Kit, so that when Thady insists on doing so he is being absurd; equally it is impossible not to sympathize with Sir Condy, particularly when his opponents are the family of his flighty wife, and Jason Quirk. The effect of the closing episode is therefore to change the reader's attitude towards Thady's loyalty. The book ends with a totally different meaning from the one with which it began. The pathetic circumstances of the generous Sir Condy's death, almost alone and unmourned at his own gate, makes it possible to read *Castle Rackrent* as a not unsympathetic account of the passing of old-fashioned landlordism.

This was just what the Edgeworths were afraid of. They were gratified by the tale's instant success. "My father asked for "Belinda", "Bulls", &c, found they were in good repute — "Castle Rackrent" in better — the others often borrowed, but "Castle Rackrent" often bought."[22] It went into five English editions before inclusion in the first Collected Works, and for several years after its appearance the Edgeworths would hear stories of how it was read and enjoyed in high places. "We hear from good authority that the king was much pleased with Castle Rack Rent — he rubbed his hands & said what what — I know something now of my Irish subjects."[23] During his visit to London in 1805 Edgeworth also learnt that "Mr. Pitt is a great admirer of Castle RR —& Lord Carhampton says it is the best book he had read since he learnt to read."[24]

Just the same they were worried that it would be resented by the Irish themselves, especially if the limited vision and mistaken loyalty of Thady was not taken ironically, while his picture of the

Rackrents was accepted as an up-to-date description of the Irish gentry. One acquaintance did object to it as a travesty, but most people in their own circle tactfully assured them that it was "a representation of past manners that should flatter the present generation."[25] Mrs. Edgeworth asked her brother William, who had a Church living near Cork, to find out how it was received there. His reply shows that many people were reading it as a "straight" account of present-day Irish society, and in fact liked it or disliked it with that criterion in mind.

> One *lady* told me she did not like it at all because it was so severe and she feared so true a satire on her dear country — Another who is a native in the West Indies & never lived above a couple of years in Ireland said it was 'very entertaining sure' — but as to being a picture of the manners of Ireland, that was nonsense 'for I never saw nothing like it' — a revd. gentleman said the other day that it was not in the least a true picture of Irish manners, '& how should it? — for I hear the author is some low fellow that never was in Ireland in his life & evidently does not know how to write' — But except by these, I have heard it exceedingly admired both 'as a picture of Irish squires' 'as a piece of good satirical writing' — 'a good imitation of the style of the narrator' — and as 'an entertaining tale'.[26]

This letter justifies the anxiety the Edgeworths had felt. The fact that Thady has as it were captured *Castle Rackrent*, and successfully imposed his personality upon it, is evidence of Maria's great gift for characterization, and her remarkable powers of filling out a portrait through the nuances of speech. On the other hand the tale as a whole is at odds with itself, and at odds with Maria. The ironic message of the first half is cancelled out by the pathos of the second. The result is that *Castle Rackrent* has always been taken to mean the opposite of what the Edgeworths believed: that the passing of thoroughly selfish and irresponsible landlords is to be regretted when they come from a native Irish family and can command a feudal type of loyalty from some of their peasants.

MARIA EDGEWORTH AND THE ENGLISH NOVEL[1]

Ernest Baker

Thanks to a happy chronological accident, a bridge was provided from the eighteenth century to the nineteenth in the work of two novelists, Maria Edgeworth and Jane Austen, who belonged to both the old and the new age. Without any shock of surprise or startling change of scenery, we gradually find that the past has been left behind and we are entering upon the present. There are still many features in the scenes brought before the eye which are now obsolete or quaint and old-fashioned. But compare any of their novels with *Pamela* and *Joseph Andrews,* the second centenary of which will be celebrated a few years hence — the Victorians hardly noticed the first. There the world depicted is not our world; all is remote and unfamiliar, except the general traits that are of our own race and kindred or simply human and of all ages. It is a world seemingly more than four times as far removed as that of Miss Edgeworth and Miss Austen, whose early novels, nevertheless, including their finest, were written only half a century later. In *Castle Rackrent* perhaps, but certainly not in *Tales of Fashionable Life, Sense and Sensibility,* or *Pride and Prejudice,* do the manners seem strange or antiquated; still less is there in the bearing and workmanship of the novelist that requires the reader to make allowances.

For the differences between the two groups of novels are in the social physiognomy rather than in the mode of portrayal. The fashion of the world had changed much more than the fashion of novel-writing. In these fifty years, there had been an unexampled advance in order and civilization. England had never been so quiet for so long a space, never more prosperous. The middle classes were merging with the upper classes, in spite of the deference and even obsequiousness paid as much as ever to rank and title; they were in possession of wealth, comfort, and leisure, and were now the most stable element in the community, the portion that was coming more and more to represent the intelligence, the morality and refinement of the nation. Incidentally, they formed the reading public, which was now large enough to make the fortune of a successful novelist. Even the minor novels show clearly the amelioration of manners, the new interests shaping life, the steady transformation of society from centre to circumference, and the gradual suppression of the differences between town and country so far as the more cultivated classes were concerned. In both Miss Edgeworth's and Miss Austen's novels, the stage is oftener a manor-house or a vicarage than the fashionable end of the metropolis, and changes of scene from London or Bath to the country are a very small change of environment. The process of rapid evolution with its reactions upon literature which can be followed in the history of fiction better than anywhere else had completed a definite stage. Actually, it was to go on at an accelerated pace throughout the nineteenth century, till now, when a state of transition seems to be the normal state of mankind. But in essentials the society that we meet in the novels of these two ladies is that of our own contemporaries.

It would be misleading, however, not to make large allowances for the point of view and the different radius of vision of the older and the younger novelists. Simply to contrast Fielding's and Richardson's view of the world with that of Miss Edgeworth and Miss Austen would be to exaggerate the real disparity between the two epochs. Novelists latterly had shown a tendency to confine themselves to those educated classes who read their books. These two ladies kept almost exclusively to their own class; they rarely went outside a limited sphere in which manners and morals were more refined than in any other section of society. Fielding, on the other hand, had been catholic in his range, and never afraid to tell the truth however ugly; he drew his characters from low as well as from high life, as he often stops to point out, and rivalled Hogarth in his insistence on the barbarism of the mob. Even Richardson left in his two chief novels a distorted impression of a lawless state of society by choosing transgressions of the established code for his dramatic material. Fanny Burney, whose novels and letters are on the whole good evidence for the progress of manners at a half-way stage, had for the sake of sensation given some slight glimpses of the vice and brutality of the lower classes, though her chief object was to make fun of the absurdities of those who aped their betters or of the crazes and affectations rampant in a more elevated sphere. But she could have known very little at first hand about the lower classes; she was a woman, like her two successors, with a woman's narrow experience. Maria Edgeworth did not by any means overlook the poorer classes in her Irish stories, as will be seen; but she saw them as one of their superiors, at the best as a charitable observer, not as one who could even in imagination make herself one of them. All three, in short, gave the feminine view of life; they were not qualified to do more, and their delicacy would have shrunk from a candid treatment of many things that could not escape their notice. It needed a man, a Walter Scott, with an eye like Fielding's for all sorts and conditions, to restore the balance, as he did in the novels of his own day or of his yesterday which are the nearest approach to the broad survey of his predecessor. And even Scott is to be read as an historian of society only if some correction is applied for the romantic bias even in his semi-contemporary pictures. He was determined to entertain and enthral, no matter if the exact truth of his version of reality suffered. Thus a great many disturbing factors have to be taken into account if a register of the changes of the last fifty years is sought in the novels.

Miss Edgeworth and Miss Austen found their right medium in the domestic novel, that form of the novel of manners the general scheme of which had evolved and come into chief favour during the last half-century. Fielding's vivid rendering of life as it goes quietly or impetuously on was here applied to a narrower expanse, and was blended as occasion served with Richardson's closer scrutiny of the heart and with his systematic moralism. Both were clear-headed enough to avoid the uncertainty of aim and halting craftsmanship which had rendered the majority of recent novels so glaringly inferior to the pattern set by the illustrious four. They recovered the lost ground. For there was no affectation of any kind in either of them. They wrote simply and sincerely, with a definite and consistent attitude of mind that kept them to the point. Both were writers because they had to be, and were not, as too many of the literary tribe, mercenaries, gushing amateurs, propagandists in disguise, or mere charlatans. Jane Austen wrote to amuse herself; Maria Edgeworth as a practical teacher, whose strong sense of responsibility impelled her to correct and advise the rash and erring. To her, fiction was one of the useful arts; only once did she yield to the joy of unfettered creation, when she bent the inner ear to listen to old Thady "dictating" the history of Castle Rackrent.

Both were writing in the period of the Romantic movement; but they were both untouched by it, and no doubt were unaware that any such thing as an important literary revolution was going on. Both were well read in English literature, but their culture was that

of the eighteenth century. They knew there was a poet named
Wordsworth; he visited the Edgeworths in Ireland; but their
acquaintance with his poetry was evidently very slight, and neither
had an inkling of his inner meaning. Coleridge they had hardly
heard of, and Keats and Shelley never appeared on the horizon
even to Maria Edgeworth, who outlived these younger poets.
Crabbe was much more to their taste, as to that of most readers in
what we now call the age of romance. Miss Edgeworth was more
interested in people than in books, and among the writers whom
she loved not many were poets. She read Scott's lays and novels
with enthusiasm, very different from Jane Austen's lukewarm
appreciation of the first Waverley novels, the only ones she lived to
read.[2] But Scott was romantic without participating in the new
romanticism; and it was his rich humanity, the truth and
splendour of his dramatization of both present and past, and his
discovery "that facts are better than fiction, that there is no
romance like the romance of real life,"[3] that fascinated Maria
Edgeworth. She herself had a weakness for romance of the old
stamp, in spite of her ridicule of sentimentalism and of Gothic and
other extravagances. The truth is that the deeper romanticism, the
romanticism of Wordsworth and his fellows, did not enter fully into
English fiction until the time of the Brontë sisters, with their deep-
rooted sense of a material world transfused with spirit. Those
novelists who were the contemporaries of Wordsworth and
Coleridge, Shelley and Keats, reveal not the slightest consciousness
of that awakening of the soul and imagination which was of its very
essence.

Maria Edgeworth (1767-1849) has some affinity with the school
of Bage, Holcroft, and Godwin, in that she embodied a social
philosophy in a series of novels and tales; she might almost be
considered as the last and best of that group. But she was not, like
them, speculative and polemical; and she was not in the habit of
talking at large about the abstract principles which she applied to
the daily predicaments of practical life. As to political questions,
she left them to other people. Her own mind was made up. In
truth, she was not a profound thinker: but she was an intelligent
woman, the daughter of an able man, Richard Lovell Edgeworth,
and the friend of Ricardo and of Étienne Dumont, colleague and
expositor of Jeremy Bentham.[4] On the whole, she had a clearer
and more consistent view of the social order than was attained by

the revolutionary school in all their exposures of injustice, their sentimental contrasts of selfishness and virtue, and their incessant discussions of ethical and political problems in the light of soaring but ill-defined ideals. Whilst they harped upon the rights of man, she and her father were content to point out his duties. Bentham, it will be remembered, likewise denied that the individual had inherent rights, even the right to equality. In effect, their insistence on what every man owes to the community, his obligation to make himself useful to his fellows, is nothing else than Bentham's utilitarianism, the doctrine of the greatest good of the greatest number, of the subservience of each to all, the identification of doing right with social service.

For it would be illusory to suppose that Maria Edgeworth had already grasped the modern conception of the individual as a member of the human family, a function in a living organism, the idea that was soon to displace the mechanical notion which had dominated the minds and circumscribed the imagination both of novelists and of politicians and social reformers. If she ever caught glimpses of this deeper view, its full significance had not dawned upon her. The eighteenth century beheld society merely as a vast aggregation of similar individuals, the arithmetical sum of many equal units, whose position in the social scheme was settled for them, not by personal differences, but by the external accidents of rank, property, privilege, or the inferior lot inherited by the majority.[5] This basic assumption had become instinctive; this was how men thought, how they looked at the world, until the end of the eighteenth century. Defoe and Richardson would have the individual accept resignedly his subjection to the appointed order; the revolutionary novelists would have him rebel and assert his claim to freedom and happiness. Both parties, nevertheless, acquiesced in the same fundamental axiom of the relation of the one to the many.

It is impossible to say at what precise date novelists and others began to think in different terms, though it can be safely asserted that the new view did not become general in fiction until romanticism came in with the Brontës. Then it is that characters are overheard demanding: "What was I created for? What is my place in the world?"[6] It is the view which has prevailed until the event of the present day, when it is being challenged as an inadequate scheme for the realization of a complete personal life, and its corollary, progress, for every progress, is seen to be meaningless. Today personality is felt to be a higher object than any social organization, and it is being recognised that all institutions, including the State itself, exist for the service of personality. Yet Burke's prescient vision of the nation as a living structure,[7] ever developing, and not a mere mechanical sum of identical units, was fruitful in giving a deeper significance to history, as well as a warning to such rash reformers as thought it an easy task to overthrow the fabric and rebuild it from the foundations up. The full conception of the social system as an organism, and of the individual members as each exercising a vital function in the general service, was animating to the sociologist, the moral philosopher, and the novelist. Virtue, integrity, and happiness were thus seen to correspond to the fulfilment of that for which each was fitted; vice was failure and disobedience. Towards some such answer to the social engima Bage, Holcroft, and Godwin had striven according to their lights; but they were more troubled by the breakdown of the old philosophy than ready with a comprehensive and satisfactory one to put in its place, in spite of the genial, optimism of the first two and the perfectibilian theories of the last. They complacently responded to the revolutionary cry of liberty, equality, fraternity, though it was only a sentimental expression of the old individualism.

If Maria Edgeworth was too conservative to be prepared to see men and women all as organs of the body politic, with functions to perform for the common good, she had at any rate a healthy conviction of their duties and responsibilities. She herself belonged to the ruling classes, the classes which up to the time of her entry upon middle age were, in Ireland, unmistakably rulers. She never divested herself of some prejudices in regard to rank and station, and often in her edifying tales for children seems to be simply bidding them do that which is proper to the state of life to which Providence has called them. But her utilitarianism was an adequate working plan. She was not an unenlightened person, and had a right apprehension of the good of society as a whole. The general happiness, social service, the call of duty rather than the assertion of rights, are the ideas implicit in all her stories, whether nursery fables inculcating the social virtues or full-length novels, "tales of fashionable life," for the admonishment and education of the adult.

Her own duty was evident; her function, if she had so regarded it, had been marked out for her by her upbringing and special abilities. As clearly as her father, she saw that the principal need of all classes was education, with a view to the cheerful and efficient performance of their duties in the world. Her mission was to be a teacher, and she carried out her task with zeal and conscientiousness. Now and then she did still better. Moved unawares by the impulse to express herself, to realize her personality, a thing for which there was really no place in her philosophy, for it was the dictate of genius which is ruled by no philosophy, she wonderingly obeyed. She wrote *Castle Rackrent* without even knowing how she did it. And, again, in many parts of *The Absentee* and *Ormond* she built better than she knew. Partly, no doubt, it was the Irish inspiration that seized her; she always wrote best and most easily when the theme was Irish. And thus she was the first writer to render the racial peculiarities of the Irish with the charm of perfect comprehension, although, like Swift, Goldsmith, and Henry Brooke, she was only an adopted child of the country. Her first distinction is, then, to stand foremost among didactic novelists, her second to be the author of the finest Irish story ever written, her third to have given new shape and importance to the short story. This had been the immemorial pattern for fiction with a lesson to propound, and she had a recent model in the *Contes moraux* of Marmontel, whose general level of accomplishment was indeed higher than hers.[8] But a comparison must not be pressed; her aims were so different that comparison loses its point. Among her tales for the young are many small masterpieces of neat workmanship and sympathetic imagination. The more expansive stories of the world in which men and women live out their destinies are not intrinsically superior, but they too helped to re-establish and renovate a form of fiction in which the moderns have excelled.

AN EARLY 'IRISH' NOVELIST[1]

W. B. Coley

As its running title clearly implies, *Castle Rackrent* is in some ways more like a tale than like what today would be recognized as a full-fledged novel. It is short. It is narrated or told by a person. And it has considerable affinity for what in American literature would be called the tall tale. Furthermore, the flavour of the book is extremely anecdotal. In her Preface Miss Edgeworth takes some pains to defend what she saw as a prevailing public taste for anecdote. She supports such a taste against the tory critical charges that it was trivial and low and in doing so links the fact of anecdote to the much larger issue of verisimilitude in literature. The novel, we see clearly today, has always had an interesting, if shifting, relationship to history. From the very beginning the claims of fiction to deal with the real world have been measured, often invidiously, against those of its supposedly more literal sister activity. Unlike poetry, in its modern phases at least, the novel has had to contend with the problem of realism on many fronts. The novel's bulk, its very prosaicness, its slowness, these and other characteristics have somehow made the genre more vulnerable to charges that it was not getting at reality. We have only to review the eighteenth-century precursors of Miss Edgeworth to see how often their novels masquerade as Lives, Histories, Histories of Lives, and the like. As her own preface makes clear, to write fiction was to write history. History of a very special sort, to be sure, for in her view most professional or public historians wrote impossibly fanciful and inflated history. She argues that the best, the most genuinely instructive history takes the form of secret memoirs, private anecdotes, familiar letters, the careless, even unfinished conversations of domestic, not public, life. Her preference for documents like these seems to have had two important corollaries for her larger view of fiction itself. First, she believed in collecting the "most minute facts relative to the domestic lives, not only of the great and good, but even of the worthless and insignificant." Minuteness and particularity were not exactly staples of most eighteenth-century novels, as we hardly need Dr. Johnson's streaky tulip to remind us. Nor are they exactly staples of *Castle Rackrent*, as it turns out, for the very brevity of that work precludes the sort of density of detail which marks and sometimes disfigures her later work. On the other hand, the relatively few "facts" which *Castle Rackrent* supplies are indeed minute in the sense of trivial and informal and domestic. And these charactertistics remind us of Miss Edgeworth's notion that the novel as history ought to turn away from the public and pompous toward the private and simple, toward what the sensibility of a later day would call "the little person." As the professional historian can hardly be bothered with the private circumstances even of public figures, to say nothing of the private circumstances of the poor and unimportant, it is to the biographer that we must turn for the truth that lies behind the scenes.

A second corollary of Miss Edgeworth's view of the proper business of the historian-biographer is that the latter succeeds in inverse proportion to the extent that he intellectualizes or makes literary his productions. "A plain unvarnished tale is preferable to the most highly ornamented narrative." An antirhetorical doctrine this, a call for simplicity. And in *Castle Rackrent* the call is heeded. Miss Edgeworth goes through all the old business of pretending that the book is in fact the memoirs of "an illiterate old steward" of the family that owned the castle. Like Defoe, Swift, and a raft of her lesser predecessors, she pretends the publication of the book is owing to an editor, whose function it is to write down the narrator's account and to provide the ignorant English reader with explanatory notes and glossings of difficult Irish terms. In these somewhat technical respects *Castle Rackrent* is well within the familiar conventions of fiction. Less conventional, however, is the placement of the narrator within the book. In eighteenth-century narrative fiction the tendency was to put the narrator in the centre of his narrative, that is, to make him the narrator of his own life or his own experiences. Moll Flanders and Lemuel Gulliver, for example, function as autobiographers. On the other hand, Thady Quirk, the illiterate narrator of *Castle Rackrent*, tells the story not of his own life but of the family which he was born and bred to serve. He functions as both a participant and an observer and in this sense is more like Nick Carraway of *The Great Gatsby* than he is like Lemuel Gulliver. There is at least one important gain for fiction in this more sophisticated handling of the narrator. No longer need the reader's view of things be utterly dependent on and exactly coextensive with the narrator's view of things. We depend to a considerably degree upon what Thady Quirk discloses, but our final estimate of the meaning of his disclosures must also take into account the fact that it is Thady who is making the disclosures. That there is a problem of perspective here which is missing in most earlier fiction can be demonstrated by comparing the sometimes binocular effects of *Castle Rackrent* with the unremitting flatness of the narrative in *Moll Flanders*.

Perhaps Miss Edgeworth's most celebrated contribution to the history of the novel is her creation of what can be called a genuinely *regional* locale. *Castle Rackrent* has in fact been called the first regional novel in English, a statement which, though it may raise all the old doubts about questions of primacy, deserves to be pondered. Until Edgeworth and Scott the novel in English was not much interested in region as such. For one thing, neoclassical aesthetics did not encourage the treatment of place in so detailed and specific a way as to make regional effects possible. Fielding may have composed *Tom Jones* with the aid of a map and an almanac, but whatever new verisimilitude this may have effected was largely topographical. Erase the place names in Fielding and you have no idea where you are. *Humphry Clinker*, to take one more case, undertakes to describe Scotland and the Scots, especially Edinburgh and its people, but it would be an act of the sheerest partiality to argue that Smollett thereby created much of a sense of region. Ireland, one might retort, cries out for regional treatment. Perhaps. But where in the considerable Anglo-Irish literature of the seventeenth and eighteenth centuries do we find it so treated? Gothic novels are often cited for their contribution to fiction's sense of setting, but the setting of a Gothic novel depends for its effect on an absence of any recognizable resemblance to real places living or dead. Therefore, perhaps Miss Edgeworth's primacy in this respect has merit. Scott at least thought so. In the postscript to *Waverley* (1814), which has itself been called the first *historical* novel, he speaks of having drawn inspiration from the Irish portraits in the work of Miss Edgeworth.

At this point it seems sensible to make a tentative distinction between the regional novel and the historical novel, between, that is, Miss Edgeworth and Scott. Properly speaking, the regional novel does two things which are vital to any conception of it. First, it creates a sense of reciprocity between persons and places such that we no longer see the isolated stage Irishman, for example, that buffoon of farce, but an aggregate of persons living together in some sort of distinct society or culture. This society or cultural grouping ought to give us a genuinely autochthonous sense of having sprung from the very ground or region it is described as inhabiting, taking on the colouration of its habitat, so to speak, and in turn effecting certain changes in that habitat by virtue of certain characteristics acquired from it. Fielding describes Joseph Andrews as an *autokopros*, literally, sprung from a dunghill, but no one has ever seriously maintained that Joseph was therefore a regional type. Fielding does not bother to establish any integral relation between the hero and the specifics of his habitat. Joseph in fact transcends his dunghill and thereby transcends geography and region. For Miss Edgeworth, however, the dunghill makes a difference. It produces distinctive offspring known as Irish, and these in turn treat their dunghill in a way that is distinctive and Irish. Which leads us to the second thing the regional novel must do. It must create a region or a world that is recognizably like some region or part of the nonfictional world. Ireland, for example, or Wessex, or the American Middle West, or Yoknapatawpha county. It is this second requirement of the definition which excludes the Gothic novel from taking its place with the regional novel.

The historical novel would appear to derive, at least in part, from the regional novel, in that it too requires the capacity to present a world identifiable in both place and time, a society with characteristics that are more than merely the reiteration of certain type characters inhabiting it. This capacity the historical novel could have found already suggestively employed in the regional novels of Miss Edgeworth, as Scott amiably asserted he had found it in *Castle Rackrent*. In *Waverley*, of course, Scott gives us more than just a study of a society or of a world. He retrieves a time sufficiently remote or seemingly remote from his own that it can be called a historical time. And he endows it, though vanished, with the same kind of plausibility that the regional novelist achieved for certain pockets of a world which, although not literally contemporary, does not quite strike us as past either. Time in the sense of pastness, then, is one of Scott's contributions to what he found already available; and history, too, in the sense of a notion of causality, the interdependence of events previously seen either as timeless or as merely having sequence. Neither of these two concepts — pastness and history — seems quite to have been within Miss Edgeworth's grasp as a writer. Although *Castle Rackrent* contains several editorial assertions that it deals with "other times," that the manners it represents are "not those of the present age," the objective reader may well feel that pastness is not achieved by such assertions or by claiming that the fictional date of the work is 1782. And yet, Miss

Edgeworth's common theme is the effect of the past upon the present, particularly as manifested in lingering and ineffective traditions or ingrained cultural habits. Still, a backward look of twenty years or so is nothing to the nineteenth-century novelist. So short a backward look tests fully neither the precision of the novelist's historical memory nor his powers of wholesale retrieval of what he has remembered. And to treat the past as present in the present is really not the same thing as making a plausible reconstruction of a bygone era. To be sure, Miss Edgeworth is more actuely aware of the past and its effects than, say, Fielding. When Fielding credits the lawyer in *Joseph Andrews* with having been alive "these four thousand years," he is choosing to be ahistorical, to cut his character off from normal space-time, to universalize him, as it were. In *Castle Rackrent*, at least, Miss Edgeworth does no such thing. Her characters seem clearly located in both time and place. It is simply that compared to Scott's, they strike us as insufficiently past.

The assertion is sometimes made that the historical novel must deal with great public (i.e., historical) events. To put it another way, this kind of novel must establish a serious interrelation between the fictional and the historical events that take place in it. If we apply such a criterion rigorously, we cannot call *Castle Rackrent* a historical novel. As she made clear in her Preface, Miss Edgeworth held little brief for the historian who dealt in public events or historical occasions. She thus takes her place in that great shift in the attitude of the novel toward the private and the trivial, so brilliantly elucidated in Auerbach's *Mimesis*. On the other hand, by all but excluding recognizable historical occasions from her book she may have prevented herself from accomplishing the historical novel. Our imagination doubtless warms to think of her hard at work on her requiem of the Protestant Ascendancy while the Rising of 1798 eddied about her very doors, but the hard fact is that in Thady Quirk's narrative there is scarcely a whisper about the background of Irish history. One can retort that it takes more than the mere presence or absence of historical events to make or break, as it were, a historical novel. Part of *Tom Jones*, for example, takes place against the specific background of the Scottish rebellion of 1745. Yet there is a world of difference between Fielding's treatment of the Forty-five and Scott's. In *Tom Jones* the Forty-five bears about the same relation to the events played off against it as the topography or meteorology of Tom's journey to London bears to the events of that journey. The relation in these cases is more or less a matter of plausibility, of verisimilitude. In Scott's *Waverley,* on the other hand, the Forty-five is shown to be in some sense both a cause and an effect of the events Scott chooses to write about. Today we should call such a relationship "organic," and we would probably not consider that Miss Edgeworth had quite got it. However, to harp thus on her supposed defects is to insist that she be a kind of novelist she in fact is not. Perhaps we would do better to sum up her historical importance by reminding ourselves that she did much to prepare the way for Scott and possibly Turgenev, to teach the nations in their greater name, as it were, and thus can be said to have helped change the sensibility of an age, a function not given to many to perform.

THE NATURE OF THE IRISH NOVEL[1]

Thomas Flanagan

Nineteenth-century Ireland was a land splintered by divided loyalties and ancient hatreds. Sir Walter Scott, visiting the country in 1825, noted with some contempt: "Their factions have been so long envenomed, and they have such narrow ground to do their battle in, that they are like men fighting with daggers in a hogshead."[2] Much later Yeats, writing as an Irishman and in bitterness, would make the same point:

Out of Ireland have we come.
Great hatred, little room,
Maimed us at the start.
I carry from my mother's womb
A fanatic heart.[3]

One is tempted to seize upon these quotations as epigraphs to a study of Irish fiction, for most Irish novels accept as given the condition to which they point. The English novelist was concerned with social choice and personal morality, which are the great issues of European fiction. But to the Irish novelist these were subordinated to questions of race, creed, and nationality — questions which tend of their nature to limit the range and power of fiction. Yet for the Irishman these were the crucial points by which he was given social identity.

If the social pattern was much more various than is generally supposed, the popular notion of a dual society, the masters and the ruled, has a large measure of truth. On one side stood "native" Ireland. It had become a nation of peasants, fiercely Catholic, indifferent or hostile to statute law, Gaelic-speaking or at least heavily influenced by the traditions of Gaelic society, nourished by dark and sanguinary resentments and aspirations. On the other side stood the nation of the Anglo-Irish, land-owning, Protestant, and, of course, English-speaking. Though this nation aspired, intermittently, to political independence, in point of fact, its culture and its modes of thought were indisputably English.

The Irish novelists, being men of their generation, realized that the two nations were yoked in a common fate, that despite all hatreds and blood-letting they would have to endure each other. And yet, when all the fair words had been spoken, each writer would find himself pledged to his own people. Maria Edgeworth might reach gropingly, in her last novels, to Gaelic Ireland, but she remained a lady of the Big Houses, anxious for peace, but for peace upon the terms imposed by the Big Houses. And Gerald Griffin, for all the liberality of his sentiments, was haunted by his vision of that older Ireland which existed before the Big Houses, and which remained incarnate in the shattered Norman keeps of the Geraldines. Each novelist was forced to pose to himself the question of what Ireland was and of what it meant to be an Irishman. From tensions of this kind the Irish novels derive their strength.

The Irish novelist, like any writer, was quarrelling with himself and with his culture. A special and distinguishing circumstance obtained, however. The quarrel was addressed, in the first instance, not to his own people but to strangers, and it was usually couched in the language of explanation. That is to say, most of the Irish novels were addressed to an English audience, and most of them offered to explain and interpret the sister kingdom. The supposed "editor" of the history of *Castle Rackrent* places his story "before the English reader as a specimen of manners and characters, which are perhaps unknown in England. Indeed the domestic habits of no nation in Europe were less known to the English than those of their sister country, till within these few years."[4] Nor is this novel an exception; of the fiction which we shall be considering, only the early stories of William Carleton were written directly for an Irish audience. And Carleton's stories, when collected and published as a book, were preceded by a note in which the author acknowledged the English reading public as his probable audience.[5]

This circumstance had a decisive effect upon the aims and purposes of the Irish novel. Numberless prefaces, forewords, and introductions make the same tedious avowal of intentions. Ireland, so much statements may be summarized, is for the first time to be represented "as it really is," and in a spirit free of religious and political rancour. Lady Morgan, an inveterate offender in this regard, tells us in the preface to *O'Donnel* that her tale is devoted to "the purposes of conciliation, and to incorporate the leaven of favourable opinion with that heavy mass of bitter prejudice, which writers, both grave and trifling, have delighted to raise against my country."[6] She assures us in the preface to *Florence Macarthy* that her aim throughout her career has been "to sketch the brilliant aspect of a people struggling with adversity, and by the delineation of national virtues, to excite sympathy, and awaken justice."[7] Griffin and Carleton, better and less didactic writers, make similar avowals. And since Richard Lovell Edgeworth, who supplied the introductions to his daughter's novels, was a professional moralist, his remarks may be entrusted to the reader's imagination.

The "editor" of *Castle Rackrent* spoke sober truth: the English reader knew less of Ireland than he did of most European countries. What little he did know was unpleasant. Some hideous insurrection would remind him of its existence, or a reckless Ascendancy duellist would cause a day's gossip. The Act of Union, however, made Ireland a matter of direct concern, and the English public was soon burdened with the rumours of agrarian outrage and armed conspiracies which had hitherto been swallowed by the silences of Dublin Castle. Then, in the eighteen twenties, the mass agitation for the removal of the Penal Laws gave evidence of what was to become a recurrent problem: Ireland's ability to provoke a parliamentary crisis.

There was a general desire for information about Ireland, and an interest in the nature of Irish society. Novels were then considered proper vehicles of such information, and writers rushed into print with accounts of "Ireland today." Orange novelists like the aptly named George Brittaine came forward with sombre chronicles of brutish priest-ridden peasants held in check by a devout garrison of British Christians. Catholic writers like John Banim replied in kind. And liberal Protestants attempted a judicious adjustment of the two extreme positions — a task which was to find more favour in English than in Hibernian eyes. The atmosphere was charged with political passions, and every Irish writer, no matter how far removed he may have been from such concerns, knew that his picture of Ireland would be scanned for its political overtones.

Nor was Catholic Emancipation the only issue which could enmesh the novelist in controversy. The peasant question, the questions of land and of absenteeism are all represented in the novels of the period. All of these, however, came to be overshadowed, in the final decade of the half century, by the single issue of the repeal of the Act of Union, which would mean, of course, the restoration of Irish nationality. The Edgeworths were supporters of the Union, although Richard Lovell, for reasons peculiar to his temperament, had cast his vote against it in the Irish Parliament. And Ireland's claim to nationhood is the chief theme in Lady Morgan's fiction. The issue became one of wide public concern, however, only with the revival of O'Connell's agitation and with the founding of *The Nation* in 1842.

Thus the Irish novel, in one of its aspects, can be termed a kind of advocacy before the bar of English public opinion. In plot and in characterization it often served the interests of special pleading. Maria Edgeworth's scrupulous landlords, venal agents, and irresponsible peasants, like John Banim's oppressed and unwilling rebels and conspirators, are too carefully posed for the vindication of a thesis to constitute a representation of Ireland "as it really was." This propagandistic bent of the Irish novel is its weakest point. That it performed successfully the services of propaganda is doubtful. Very likely the contrasting and conflicting images of Ireland cancelled each other out. The major writers, however much they may have differed, saw Irish experience as being essentially tragic, and this is the one view which English readers were not prepared to accept. The reading public much preferred the Ireland of Charles Lever — an enchanting and dowdy land of *dolce far niente,* in which dashing dragoons and impoverished fox hunters held genial sway over a mob of feckless rustics.

Irish novels were invariably reviewed by British journals on the assumption that they had been written to please English taste or to shape English opinion. John Wilson Croker's slashing attacks upon Lady Morgan in the pages of *The Quarterly Review* were inspired by his fear of the damage which her novels might do to the high-Tory position which claimed his own slippery allegiance. Similarly it was to England that the Irish writer looked for critical judgment. In only a few instances, such as Carleton's remarks upon the novels of Banim and Lever, Thomas Davis's review of Carleton's own work, or an occasional article in *The Dublin University Magazine,* is criticism from contemporary Irish sources relevant or important.

The dependence of Irish writers on an English audience did not seem at all exceptionable. London, after all, was indisputably the intellectual and literary capital of the British Isles. The problem, rather, is to define the sense in which their work may properly be called Irish. This problem, which is enmeshed in old and barren controversies and clouded over by doctrinaire political and cultural assumptions, inevitably confronts the student of the literature of nineteenth-century Ireland.

Irishmen, to be sure, had made generous contributions to the literature of the two preceding centuries — Swift, Congreve, Farquhar, Sheridan, Goldsmith, and Burke were all Irish. Except for Swift, however, who in this as in all things is a law unto himself, the fact of Irish birth is irrelevant to their accomplishments. Children of the English garrison, they took quick and natural root in English soil. The attempts which have been made to trace out an "Ango-Irish" — let alone a "Celtic" — strain in their writings are quite unconvincing.[8] Goldsmith's friends, it is true, made a standing joke of his Irish background, and his transformation of a Roscommon village into "sweet Auburn" presents us with a literary oddity. And Burke, who was descended from one of the old Norman families and whose mother was a Roman Catholic, possessed a familiarity with Irish affairs which was to stand him in good stead. But Sheridan's Irish birth we are likely to remember only because of his name and because he was in the habit of tossing a stage-Irishman into his plays. As for Congreve — we accept the fact with mild incredulity. The same might be said of the century's only Irish novelist, Henry Brooke, the author of *The Fool of Quality* (1765-70).

There did exist in the eighteenth century a literature which was indisputably Irish — the poetry of the Gaelic hedge writers, who had inherited the traditions of Gaelic letters as fully as had Goldsmith those of English poetry. This literature was "hidden" — to employ Daniel Corkery's evocative phrase — but it was not unknown. Goldsmith himself glimpsed Turlough O'Carolan, "the last of the bards," and recorded his impressions in a brief essay.[9] It was a dying tradition, however, and might have perished without record had it not been for the retentive memory of the peasantry and the devoted labours of a few amateurs from within the garrison itself. But the development of an interest among members of the Ascendancy in the literature of the older Ireland is discussed at greater length in Chapter Eight, and need not be anticipated here. It will suffice, for the moment, to realize that high walls of language and caste separated the two cultures of eighteenth-century Ireland. Nor were these the only barriers. Brian Merriman's brilliant poem, *The Midnight Court,* is remarkable as much for the sophistication as for the antiquity of its traditional form.[10]

A single incident may bring the issue close to our own subject. In 1805 Arthur O'Neill, old and blind, sat dictating the story of his life to a clerk named Tom Hughes, who served the M'Cracken family of Belfast. O'Neill was one of the last of the race of Irish harpers, and his attachments were to that aristocratic world of the Gael which had almost vanished.

"When dinner was announced," he says, speaking of an assemblage some sixty years before, "very near a hundred of the O's and Macs took their seats. My poor self being blind, I did what blind men generally do, I groped a vacancy near the foot of the table. Such a noise arose of cutting, carving, roaring, laughing, shaking hands, and such language as generally occurs between friends, who only see each other once a year. While dinner was going on, I was hobnobbed by nearly every gentleman present. When Lord Kenmare hobnobbed me, he was pleased to say, 'O'Neill, you should be at the head of the table, as your ancestors were the original Milesians of this kingdom.'"[11]

Behind the darkened eyes of Art O'Neill, an old man talking out his life to a clerk of the family upon whose charity he depended, the Gaelic world lived and glowed in the bright colours of heraldry.

This is not surprising, for in his youth he had had another patron — Murtough Oge O'Sullivan, the half-legendary swordsman of Fontenoy and the Kerry coast. And he had crossed the sea in 1745 to play at Holyrood before Charles Edward Stuart, the "saviour and deliverer" of the Munster poets. Indeed, it has been supposed that he was present when the Irish lords met to decide whether they would risk one last throw of the dice on the Jacobite cause.[12]

O'Neill, who like all the Gaelic artists was proud to the point of snobbishness, naturally sought out the hospitality of those few titled O's and Macs who had survived the penal legislation, but he could be sure of a welcome in many a Protestant Big House. In this fashion, amicably but with little real understanding on either side, the two cultures touched one another. One such Big House is of particular interest to us. "Always," O'Neill says, "on my return from the Granard Balls, I stopped at Counsellor Edgeworth's of Edgeworthstown, where I was well received."[13] In this house ... the first and perhaps the finest of Irish narratives was written.

The "Granard Balls," which in fact were harp competitions, were held for three years running, beginning in 1781. When Lady Morgan was writing *The Wild Irish Girl*, she gathered a certain amount of information concerning the famous harpers, which she incorporated in the footnotes of that curious novel. Richard Lovell Edgeworth read the novel when it appeared in 1806, and it stirred a dim and inaccurate memory. "I believe that some of the harpers you mention were at the Harpers' Prize Ball at Granard in 1782 or 1783. One female harper, of the name of Bridget, obtained the second prize; Fallon carried off the first. I think I have heard the double-headed man."[14]

In Lady Morgan's misty imagination the harpers and bards trailed clouds of Ossianic grandeur — an attitude which Edgeworth would have called damned folly. Edgeworth was a generous man, in his brisk, hard-tempered fashion, and Art O'Neill was surely received with kindness. But O'Neill was one in an endless stream of mendicants who came to the gates of the Big House at Edgeworthstown — harpers, pipers, pilgrims, prophecy-men, fiddlers. This stream troubled Edgeworth's orderly mind and stirred his conscience, but it never touched his imagination. But then neither did O'Neill truly see "the Counsellor," as he calls Edgeworth, since every gentleman must have a title, and "the Major" or "his Reverence" or "his Lordship" did not apply.

Between these two men of the eighteenth century — the friend of Murtough Oge O'Sullivan and the friend of Erasmus Darwin — there could be no communication. Maria Edgeworth shared, in part, her father's impatience with the world which Art O'Neill represented. In the pages of *The Absentee* she deals satirically with life at Kilpatrick House, which was everything that Art O'Neill expected a Big House to be — festive, improvident, and swarming with retainers and "follyers." But if she knew little of his Ireland and cared less, she understood the moral life of her own caste with an artist's piercing, intuitive understanding. Out of her knowlege she created *Castle Rackrent*.

With this novel a tradition begins, for it is the first fictional narrative of Irish life to be written in the English language. The writers who followed Maria Edgeworth display an equal concern with the Irish scene. Are their novels to be called Irish or English or, by way of ambiguous compromise, Anglo-Irish?

Douglas Hyde dismisses them in magisterial fashion from his *Literary History of Ireland,* telling us that he has "abstained altogether from any analysis or even mention of the work of Anglicised Irishmen of the last two centuries. Their books, as those of Farquhar, of Swift, of Goldsmith, of Burke, find, and have always found, their true and natural place in every history of *English* literature that has been written, whether by Englishmen themselves or by foreigners."[15] And it is true that the nineteenth-century Irish writers have found a place in English literature, but whether, like Farquhar and Goldsmith, they have found their true and natural place is another matter. In most such histories they are to be found huddled together, a worried Hibernian band, with Marryat and Surtees pressing them hard from one side and "The Imitators of Scott" from the other.

Hyde is perfectly justified in excluding them from his own work, for he is writing the history of "the literature produced by the Irish-speaking Irish." But his statement remains somewhat disingenuous, for the point upon which he insisted throughout his distinguished career was that only the literature of the "Irish-speaking Irish" was truly Irish. To the Gaelic enthusiasts of Hyde's generation Ireland's English-language literature was in every way deplorable. It was committed to the representation of Irish life in alien and unassimilable forms, and it had resigned itself to a humiliatingly "colonial" status. In its attempts to "explain" and to "show" Ireland, it was inevitably defensive in tone and attitude.

The argument rested upon false assumptions, for a culture must be judged by what it is and does, not by what it *should* be doing. If Irish culture is to be defined by the Gaelic language, we must conclude that when the last of the hedge poets died, Ireland ceased to have a culture. Long before the Church and O'Connell cast the heavy weight of their authority on the side of English, and long before famine and emigration had thinned the ranks of Irish-speakers, it had become clear that such literary and intellectual life as Ireland possessed would find expression in English.

There is no strong reason why we should not join Professor Corkery in calling this literature Anglo-Irish. And there remains considerable point to the questions which he addresses to it:

> The answer to the question: Is there an Anglo-Irish literature? must depend on what regard we have for what Synge spoke of as collaboration — without, perhaps, taking very great trouble to explore his own thought. The people among whom the writer lives, what is their part in the work he produces? Is the writer in the people's voice? Has there ever been, can there be, a distinctive literature that is not a national literature? A national literature is written primarily for its own people: every new book in it — no matter what its theme — foreign or native — is referable to their life, and its literary traits to the traits already established in its literature. The nation's own critical opinion of it is the warrant of life or death for it. Can Anglo-Irish, then, be a distinctive literature if it is not a national literature? And if it has not primarily been written for Ireland, if it be impossible to refer it to Irish life for its elucidation, for its continued existence or non-existence be independent of Irish opinion — can it be a national literature?[16]

Professor Corkery, as the reader may have inferred, is an extreme cultural nationalist, and is happiest when a work of art is Gaelic, patriotic, Catholic, and puritanical (though the latter two terms are, in the Irish context, interchangeable). Fortunately, the brilliant accomplishments of modern Irish writers have not depended for a warrant of life or death upon the official opinion of the Republic of Ireland. The warrant for the continued existence of Yeats and Joyce and Synge is in the keeping of the republic of letters, which is at once more just and more generous.

Corkery, has, however, defined somewhat inadvertently the anomalous status of the Irish literature of the nineteenth and twentieth centuries. It is a literature which has never been able to depend for its existence on Irish opinion; only rarely has it been written primarily for its own people; more rarely still has it drawn upon "traits" established in the literature. And yet it is a literature rooted in Irish life and experience, a literature which often forces us to turn for elucidation to the thought and culture of Ireland.

Whether a body of literature which must be defined in these terms may properly be called national, whether it should be spoken of as Irish or as Anglo-Irish or as Colonial are questions which might be set forth at greater length, but not, I think, with much profit. Speaking of "that literature which had no existence until towards the end of the eighteenth century," Corkery says: "In our youth and even later it used always to be spoken of as Irish literature: and this custom old-fashioned folk have not yet given up: to them, Thomas Moore's *Melodies* are still Irish Melodies."[17] I have chosen to follow the practice of these old-fashioned folk. For one thing, they seem to have an old-fashioned preference for accuracy: *Irish Melodies* is the title which Moore, however mistakenly, gave to his work. It is also true that the word "Anglo-Irish" has slippery political and social connotations. If Maria Edgeworth belonged by class and allegiance to the Anglo-Irish, Gerald Griffin most certainly did not.

The novels of nineteenth-century Ireland were always spoken of as Irish, and we may accept the term with a full and clear understanding of what it meant. To be sure, we must also bear in mind implications which were not then clear. We have a deeper sense now of the interdependence of language and culture. We can appreciate tht much which was rich and various, much which was uniquely Irish perished when Gaelic fell into disuse. O'Connell, in a remark which the Gaelic League would later make notorious, said that "although the Irish language is connected with many recollections that twine round the hearts of Irishmen, yet the superior utility of the English tongue, as the medium of all modern communications, is so great that I can witness without a sigh the gradual disuse of Irish."[18] We may agree with the judgement and yet wonder if he realized how final a sentence he was passing on much that he cherished.

We must also bear in mind the validity of certain of Corkery's strictures. A literature which seeks to vindicate and justify the culture from which it draws its being labours under a heavy burden. (Although one which announces truculently that its heroism, suffering, and ineffable purity place it beyond the need of vindication bears a much heavier one.) When these have been taken into proper account, however, and when the limitations and particular merits of each novelist have been recognised, it becomes clear that the major Irish novelists were engaged upon a subtle and profound study of a complicated and self-contradictory society.

CASTLE RACKRENT[1]

Thomas Flanagan

Castle Rackrent is that rare event, an almost perfect work of fiction. It is a passionate, elegiac novel, muted and sardonic in tone. In one sense it is less like the novels of its own day than of our own, for all the "set scenes" are deliberately thrown away, and the acts and statements are ambiguous and unsettling. And this is appropriate to its purpose, which is to bring to life, by plot and symbol, a society which was destroyed by self-deception.

It purports to be an account, dictated by an illiterate servant named Thady M'Quirk, of the fortunes of four generations of the Rackrent family, which has ceased to exist in name, though not, perhaps, in blood. Thady is a partisan of the family, or rather, of "the honour of the family." Only when the story is finished does the reader realize that Thady has his own wry view of this matter. But, even so, he does not fully understand the story which he is telling. The meaning and passion with which he instinctively invests the words "honour" and "loyalty" lead him to bring forth evidence which prompts the reader to a quite different judgement of the Rackrents.

"Monday Morning," he begins. "Having out of friendship for the family, upon whose estate, praised be Heaven! I and mine have lived rent free time out of mind, voluntarily undertaken to publish the Memoirs of the Rackrent Family, I think it is my duty to say a few words, in the first place, concerning myself" (7).

Every line of his narrative requires either a gloss or a challenge: to the Irish peasant, only Monday morning could see a task auspiciously begun. "Rent free" sounds pleasant enough, but was the technical term for a special kind of slavery.

To look at Thady in his long, tattered greatcoat you would never think of him as "the father of Attorney Quirk; he is a high gentleman, and never minds what poor Thady says . . . but I wash my hands of his doings, and as I have lived so will I die, true and loyal to the family"(8). The Rackrents have worked their own destruction, but Attorney Quirk, as we will discover, has been its instrument.

The family bears the name of Rackrent, but by blood they are O'Shaughlins. Patrick O'Shaughlin had inherited when Tallyhoo Rackrent died without issue. The novel chronicles his career and that of his successors, Sir Murtagh, Sir Kit, and Sir Condy. He came into the estates upon the condition, which he "took sadly to heart, they say, but thought better of it afterwards, seeing how large a stake depended upon it, that he should, by Act of Parliament, take and bear the sirname and arms of Rackrent" (9). Thady would have us believe that this reluctance issues from Sir Patrick's knowledge that the O'Shaughlins are "sons of the kings of Ireland." Some of the puzzles of the novel are resolved, however, if we regard this as one of his discretions. It is more likely that Patrick had had to change not merely his name but his creed, which would have seemed to the old Catholic servant the deepest dishonour . . . .

It is Thady who creates the illusion of family, out of the feudal retainer's pride in the house which he serves. But he has the retainer's practicality. He assigns Rackrents their role in the family legend in proportion as they are generous toward him or make life easy for him. In this he reflects the attitude not only of the other peasants in the novel, who turn out to a gentleman's funeral in expectation of liquor and spectacle, but also the peasants throughout Ireland, for whom the feudal ties had in fact dissolved.

But he comes at last to believe his own myth, and even, disastrously, to communicate a sense of its glamour to Condy. Condy's mind is fixed upon an improbable past of great houses and harpists and wine in golden goblets. Because of this, he comes to believe that the Rackrents are indeed an ancient family with an obligation to live honourably. The miracle is that the young man is able to give to the fantasy a kind of fitful existence. There are moments when, because of it, he is able to draw himself up and act like the son of kings. Because the Moneygawls have challenged his claims to gentility, he weds Bella without a dowry. He squanders the last of his coins on a shawl for Judy M'Quirk and gifts for her empty-eyed children.

There is a wealth of wryly observed social fact in the novel. The tactics of Murtagh Rackrent and Jason M'Quirk are case studies in the changing methods by which Irish land was managed, and Jason's character shows a shrewd understanding on Maria's part of the new class which was rising to power. She has drawn on the fondly preserved legends of many an Anglo-Irish family. (Not least upon her own, a fact which would have caused her father, had he been more wary, to tone down the history of the Edgeworths as he relates it in his *Memoirs*).[2]

But the meaning of these facts is buried deep in Thady's "plain, unvarnished tale." There is a spell upon the Rackrent family. Thady talks of this fate in terms of luck, misfortunes, banshees, spinning coins, fairy mounts, and bog berries, but it is plain. It is a remarkably sterile family. Three times bitter widows quit the castle with no other wish than to be rid of it. The family owes its origins to a triple denial, Patrick's rejection of his name, his blood, and his creed. The denial has been made for the sake of land and the money which land brings, but these, despite every frantic measure, run through their fingers.

Thady's language is thick with the terms by which land is held and exploited — abatements, pounding, canting, replevying, tithes, duty-work, notes, bills of sale, rent-rolls. Patrick defects to get land; Murtagh is crazed by his endless lawsuits; Kit is turned into a grasping landlord and a vicious husband. And Condy denies his love. None of them is really sure that the land is his — not even Condy. And all save Condy become mindless looters of their own possessions.

Gold is the dominating symbol of the novel, and the symbol is always hedged by irony. Murtagh levels a fairy mound to increase his tillage, never suspecting that such a mound might conceal gold, buried centuries before. Jessica's wealth is made vivid by her diamond and gold cross — an ornament which her own faith makes entirely inexplicable. Condy's luck runs out when he spins a coin on which he has scratched a cross.

When Richard Lovell Edgeworth returned home from his momentous errand, he dashed off a few brisk lines which he appended to the tale with which his daughter had whiled away the weeks of his absence. The Rackrents, he wrote, were vanishing from Ireland. Perhaps they would be replaced by English manufacturers, which would be all for the best (97). The nation of Ireland, in any event, had ended with the Act of Union, and he had his own buoyant hopes for the future.

But Maria saw beyond this. Her history of the Rackrent family is the history of the eighteenth century Ascendancy, generation by generation, down to poor Condy, whose pathetic belief in honour and responsibility, born of a servant's chatter, might have sufficed, if only it had come much earlier, to some Rackrent of the past. Instead, he has inherited the sins of Ireland's masters, be they named O'Shaughlin or Rackrent — or Quirk, with the "Mc" dropped off for gentility's sake. Some transaction of the dark past, however, had put a curse upon the blood. The land of this cursed family turned always to gold; the gold turned to wind. And the fine gestures of Condy Rackrent have the weightless inconsequence of nightmare. The peasants may come to his wake, but Judy M'Quirk speaks his epitaph: "Why follow the fortunes of them that have none left?"

MARIA EDGEWORTH'S *CASTLE RACKRENT*[1]

Roger McHugh

All of Maria Edgeworth's Irish novels show clearly that there was a whole world of Irish tradition and Irish feeling of which she knew practically nothing and about which she seems to have cared less. The glossary appended to *Castle Rackrent* and the numerous footnotes in her pages show that her interest in observed Irish characteristics was restricted to their *peculiarity*, and that she had little sympathy with or curiosity about the underlying modes of thought or views of life which made them individual. How much of this was due to her own nature, kindly but not sympathetic, how much to her intelligence, able but not searching, how much to the fact that she was neither born nor reared among the people, and how much to the circumstances in which her placid life passed, it is impossible to define. "She had not the power to discern the romantic adventurousness and the spiritual bitterness that united to drive the flower of Irish Catholics to continental battlefields," wrote M. C. Seton,[2] who points out that for two centuries before her time the main line of the Edgeworths had stood for Protestantism and the English connection. "She wrote of the Celtic Irish with the keen and not unkindly insight that a good mistress possesses into the virtues and foibles of her servants . . . For all that gave significance and value to the history of the Irish Celt, for all his heritage from the past, she . . . cared nothing." This is Stephen Gwynn's view,[3] with which Dr. Krans, who mentions her "busy contented life upon a conscientiously and carefully managed estate"[4] as the reason, will be found to agree.

Indeed, it is impossible not to agree with these remarks, however conscious one may be that to have disproved them Maria Edgeworth would have had to be someone else. No doubt she hoped that a change of laws in England and a change of heart in the Anglo-Irish absentees would have produced a prosperous, loyal, and contented Ireland. "When Ireland loses her identity by an union with Great Britain, she will look back with good-humoured complacency on the Sir Kits and Sir Condys of her former existence," says the preface to *Castle Rackrent*, which goes on to assure its readers that "the race of the Rackrents has long been extinct in Ireland." The words were written by Richard, who wanted to avoid treading on the Government's corns in 1800,[5] and they are largely negatived by the rackrenting characters of *Ennui* and *The Absentee*, but his daughter has echoed his sentiments in many ways. In *Ennui* insurrection is called "epidemic infection," and the sketch of Joe Kelly the "united man" is not complimentary, though there is a recognition that the "desperate wretches called defenders" have some reason for being desperate. So much for her political views. Her social outlook, of course, shared in their limitations, for if there was one thing that her favourite virtue, prudence,[6] preached to the Irish Protestant landlord class in the nineteenth century, it was the necessity of preserving their land from the dispossessed by relying on the British connection. The social reforms which Maria Edgeworth advocated must be seen in relation to this. In *The Absentee*, when the Clonbronys return to Ireland to become resident and improving landlords, the curtain falls upon a happy peasantry crying out to their beloved masters "Long may you live to rule over us!" Behind this, or behind the wretched attempts of Christy Mahon to run the estate which Glenthorn has handed over to him, are many implications with which the Irish reader will not agree; but there are many others which to her own class appeared not only radical, but revolutionary.

Yet these limitations do not provide the sole basis of criticism of her work on this issue. It is not enough to dismiss the Celt who appears in her pages as "a droll, disorderly, affectionate, pathetic creature":[7] for one reason because his circumstances live to some extent in her books, showing that he was more than that; secondly, because such characters as Brian and Grace, in *The Absentee*, have a dignity of their own. Again, her picture of the Irish must be seen in relation to those which had previously appeared in England. "It has been my object to describe those persons," wrote Scott of his Highland characters, "not by a caricatured and exaggerated use of their national dialect, but by their habits, manners, and feelings; so as in some distant degree to emulate the admirable Irish portraits drawn by Miss Edgeworth; so different from the 'Teagues' and 'dear joys' who so long, with the most perfect family resemblance to each other, occupied the drama and the novel."[8] In a letter to the novelist herself he says: "You have a merit, transcendent in my eyes, of raising your national character in the scale of public estimation."[9] We cannot dismiss these tributes. We may, if we please, turn on Scott and start defining *his* limitations, but when that is over it is still certain that Maria Edgeworth had used the "national" element in the novel in a better way than her predecessors, and had used her didactic pen to champion to some extent the rights of the Irish people. In conclusion, it is worth while reflecting that when Sheridan sent back the dramatic version of *The Absentee*, the chief reason which he gave for rejecting it was that the Lord Chamberlain would never license it owing to the disturbed state of the country.[10] This the prudent Maria had foreseen, but it is worth noting that she was at least ready to take the risk; as was Richard, who sent it.

THE SIGNIFICANT SILENCES OF THADY QUIRK[1]

Maurice Colgan

Maria Edgeworth's *Castle Rackrent*, published in 1800, has an important place in the history of the novel.

It is the first family saga, the first historical novel,[2] and the first novel to use a narrator who is a minor character, and who can therefore assess as well as describe events. This narrator, Thady Quirk, who comes from the ranks of the peasantry, is also the first to use demotic speech. Since *Castle Rackrent's* appearance, many authors, including Scott, Turgenev, Fenimore Cooper, Mark Twain and Alan Sillitoe have utilised its stylistic and technical innovations.

Despite its remarkable achievements, the novel somehow leaves readers dissatisfied, and it is not generally regarded as a great novel. It is the thesis of this paper that the reason for this is that Miss Edgeworth is unwilling or unable to inform the reader about significant political factors in the society she is describing.

In the first place, how did she come to write a work of such originality? Going from Oxfordshire at the age of fifteen to her father's Irish estate at Edgeworthstown, Miss Edgeworth was captivated by the idiom and imagination of the servants and tenantry. The anecdotes, and the personality, of the estate steward, John Langan, had a particular attraction for her, and he inspired the creation of Thady Quirk.[3]

Thady is intensely loyal to the Rackrent family, but his loyalty does not prevent him from accurately criticising their characters, mainly through the medium of irony. Of the spendthrift Sir Kit, he says, "though he had the spirit of a Prince, and lived away to the honour of his country abroad, which I was proud to hear of, what were we the better for that at home? The agent was one of your middle men, who grind the face of the poor, and can never bear a man with a hat upon his head — he ferreted the tenants out of their lives — not a week without a call for money — drafts upon drafts for Sir Kit — but I laid it all to the fault of the agent; for, says I, what can Sir Kit do with so much cash, and he a single man?"

Sir Kit marries a Jewess, and when he fails to persuade her to part with a valuable piece of jewellery, he locks her in a room for seven years. Thady justifies him in these terms: "Her diamond cross was, they say, at the bottom of it all; and it was a shame for her, being his wife, not to show more duty, and to have given it up when he condescended to ask so often for such a bit of a trifle in his distresses, especially when he all along made it no secret he married for money."[4]

Some critics have described the essential quality of Thady's narrative as "transparency", defined as "the ironic presentation of external fact in such a manner that the reader may see the truth underneath the external statement and draw his own conclusions."[5]

One of them goes on to claim that Thady has "the opportunity of observing or experiencing all that is finally relevant to the story."[6] Combined with his transparency, this opportunity should make him an accurate eye-witness to the life of eighteenth-century Ireland. Unfortunately, there is a large opaque area in the centre of the transparency — an area which covers everything relating to the colonial status of the country.

To begin with, there is Thady's account of the Rackrent family — originally named O'Shaughlin, we are told, and related to the ancient kings of Ireland. The impression is also given that their neighbours come of the same Gaelic stock: ". . . those men of the first consequence and landed estate in the country, such as the O'Neills of Ballynagrotty, and the Moneygawls of Mount Juliet's Town, and O'Shannons of New Town Tullyhog . . ."[7] As a matter of fact, by mid-century, few native landed families survived in Ireland. Like the Edgeworths themselves, most gentry were of English origin, and such a strong concentration in the vicinity of Castle Rackrent of Gaelic "survivors" calls for explanation.

The occasional references to the subject suggest an identity of religion, as well as nationality, between the Rackrents and the peasantry. There is the episode in which the maid is punished for breaking the Lent fast, although, we are told, Sir Murtagh "never fasted, not he."[8] The tone of this indicates that Sir Murtagh is a slack Catholic, not a Protestant. The same may be said of Sir Kit, for, when Thady suspects that the trouble between him and his wife is "about her being a heretic," he is told by Sir Kit's gentleman, "my master does not mind her heresies, but her diamond cross."[9]

Despite this, Sir Condy is elected to parliament, at a time when Catholics were barred from both Houses of Parliament, and did not even have the vote. If Sir Condy has been brought up as a Protestant, or has recanted, surely this is important enough to be mentioned by Thady?

The Rackrent inheritance, too, would have been dissipated long before the date of the writing of Thady's narrative, not by improvidence, drink or gambling, but by the law of gavelkind (which divided Catholic estates equally among the sons) or by the laws which enabled Catholic heirs to be disinherited.

Jason, Thady's son, originally destined by his father for the priesthood, becomes instead an attorney, although Catholics were not allowed to enter the legal profession until after Langrishe's Relief Act of 1792, and it is emphasised on the title page of *Castle Rackrent* that the story is set in the period preceding 1782.

The truth is that Thady's narrative ignores the most significant aspect of Irish life in the eighteenth century: the effects of the penal laws. The fact that they were not allowed to stand for parliament or vote would not have worried the peasantry, but the fact that Catholics were not allowed to purchase land, and were not allowed to obtain leases for longer than thirty-one years must have been an important factor in keeping many families on or below the poverty line.[10]

Behind Thady, of course, stands his creator. Inspired by the picturesque speech of the family steward to create an Irish peasant narrator, Maria Edgeworth nevertheless prevents him from expressing the traditions and sensibility of the peasantry, which would include their view of their relationship with their landlords. Some factors, like the penal laws, she ignores altogether. In the case of others, she presents a picture which obscures the realities of the Irish situation.

Thady boasts to a stranger that his family has lived under the Rackrents, "two hundred years and upwards."[11] This means that their relationship has survived the Elizabethan wars, the Cromwellian confiscations and the Restoration and Williamite settlements — an achievement which calls for comment, but no comment is forthcoming. Instead, it is presented as though it were a long-standing feudal relationship typical of an English rather than an Irish context.[12]

And Thady is not alone in taking this view. When word goes around about the success of Jason's plans to take over the estate, Thady tells us that "the people one and all gathered in greater anger against my son Jason, and terror at the notion of his coming to be landlord over them, and they cried, No Jason! No Jason! — Sir Condy! Sir Condy! Sir Condy Rackrent for ever!"[13]

The terms in which Thady rebukes Jason deserve attention: ". . . what will people think and say, when they see you living here in Castle Rackrent, and the lawful owner turned out of the seat of his ancestors . . ."[14]

How many Irish peasants at that time would have regarded their landlord as "the lawful owner"? More typical is the view expressed in the anonymous story, *Egan O'Rahilly and the Minister:* "There was a splendid green-boughed tree of great value growing for many years close by a church which the wicked Cromwell had plundered, above a spring overflowing with bright cold water, in a field of green turf which a thieving minister has extorted from an Irish gentleman; one who had been exiled across the wild seas through treachery . . . ."[15]

The issue is evaded by making the Rackrents an ancient Gaelic, Catholic family, and giving them, throughout the novel, the status and privileges of the Protestant Anglo-Irish.

The question now arises, to what extent was Miss Edgeworth conscious of her evasions in *Castle Rackrent?* There is no doubt that in the years leading up to 1800 she was aware of the need to resolve the Catholic question, and she was also aware of the colonial position of the Anglo-Irish gentry. At that time, she was very close in her opinions to her father, Richard Lovell Edgeworth, and in a letter to his sister dated 13 December, 1792, he wrote ". . . the preservation of my Estate shall never be my criterion of the part I should take in politics — My firm persuasion that Catholics should be represented numerically and without relation to property is certainly adverse to my own interest possessed as I am now of landed property by the right of Conquest. — That right has hitherto been sufficient for the common purposes and common sense of mankind — upon what foundation is another question . . . — It is my dear Sister my firm belief that the Catholics must form the present state of European politics necessarily obtain an entire participation of all the functions of Citizens."[16]

That Maria Edgeworth was capable of suppressing facts we know from her editing of her father's *Memoirs*. He had taken a liberal line on reform at the Volunteer Convention of November, 1783, and he was one of the minority of gentry who attended the much more radical Volunteer Convention in Dublin in the following year. This was also attended by Napper Tandy, Hamilton Rowan and William Drennan who were later to play leading roles in the United Irishmen. These activities of her father were played down by Maria in his *Memoirs* when she published them in 1820, and she omitted any mention of his attendance at the latter convention.[17]

In the aftermath of the French Revolution and the 1798 Rising in Ireland, radicalism had become unacceptable. *Castle Rackrent* itself was published at the end of a decade during which the British Government poured into Ireland more soldiers than were sent to fight Napoleon on the Continent, yet Miss Edgeworth's only reference to the military presence is to say "Did the Warwickshire militia ... teach the Irish to drink beer ... ?"[18]

But suppression in fiction is not so easy. Truth has a habit of asserting itself at one point or another. "Never trust the artist. Trust the tale." Lawrence's dictum is truer in its application to *Castle Rackrent* than to any other novel written this side of the Atlantic.

The suppressed fear that the dispossessed Irish might one day recover their lands, asserts itself in the apparent success of Jason. There is no question, however, of moral right in his claim to the Rackrent possessions. The moral claim is dealt with by Maria Edgeworth in her next Irish novel, *Ennui*.[19] Lord Glenthorn discovers that he is really the son of a peasant woman who substituted him for the real heir, whom she was fostering. He feels bound to make restitution, and relinquishes his title and estate to the real heir, who has been brought up as a peasant. The peasant does not enjoy life as a lord, and after a time pleads with the changeling Lord Glenthron to reassume the title and the responsibility. The message is obvious: Abstract "right" cannot work. The Anglo-Irish, although they have little moral justification for their position, have been educated to rule, and must be accepted by the people as their legitimate leaders. There is no alternative.

The literary imagination can be used in two ways; to penetrate beyond the surface impression to the depths of reality, or to escape from it. In *Castle Rackrent*, Maria Edgeworth escapes from reality. That is why, despite its significant place in literary history, it is not a great novel.

She herself let the cat out of the bag when she explained in 1834 why she had been unable to write another Irish novel after *Ormond* (1817). "It is impossible to draw Ireland as she now is in a book of fiction — realities are too strong, party passions too violent to bear to see, or to look at their faces in the looking glass."[20]

This also explains why a narrator like Thady — her most considerable technical contribution to the development of the English novel — could never be used by her again. Maria Edgeworth could no longer rely on him. After the 1835 General Election, she and her brother-in-law punished three Edgeworth tenants who had voted against the family interest, which by then was Tory, by calling in their "hanging gale," part of the rent which the tenant normally retained.[21] One of them, named Langan, belonged to the same family as the man who had inspired the creation of Thady forty years earlier. Was this another incident to be added to her list of realities that were "too strong" for fiction?

"SAID AN ELDERLY MAN ...": MARIA EDGEWORTH'S USE OF FOLKORE IN *CASTLE RACKRENT*

Dáithí Ó hÓgáin

In approaching *Castle Rackrent* as a folklorist, one is impressed by the authenticity, accuracy, and originality of Maria Edgeworth's observations of the life of the common people of Ireland at the end of the eighteenth century. In these respects, since the interest in folk customs and beliefs had not yet developed as a discipline, the author of *Castle Rackrent* is ahead of her time. Moreover, as an accomplished maker of fiction, she invests these cultural circumstances with persuasive character and social elements to render a powerful portrayal of Irish country life before the Union.

Maria Edgeworth made a courageous decision in choosing to tell the history of the Rackrent family through the mouth of the faithful old retainer, Thady Quirk, as a specimen of a social class other than her own. In eighteenth-century Ireland, this meant creating a credible representative of the Gaelic culture of the

ordinary Irish man and woman. There can be little doubt that in
Thady we find many characteristics of a person in his position in
the Ireland of the Big House. It may have been easy for readers of
the novel to regard all those not of the landlord or merchant class in
rural Ireland as types, and thus to see Thady as a representative of
the faceless mass of peasants. For Maria Edgeworth's artistic
purpose, therefore, it is enough that Thady should represent only
the servant of the Big House in close contact with its occupiers; but
he is also a subtly portrayed character revealing the keen
psychological insight of his creator.

Although Thady Quirk has an individual fascination, he also
has a distinctively native Irish cultural background. His chronicle
contains a good deal of folklore — especially folk-beliefs and folk-
customs — and Maria Edgeworth is anxious that her readers
should not miss the significance of these elements. She frequently
takes care to comment on them in the Glossary (98-114). The
Glossary also includes much social detail and explanations of
linguistic and other data, all of which she saw as further necessary
information for the reader and are developments on her skilled
attempts at providing the narrative with a particular, observed
cultural setting. In view of all this, *Castle Rackrent* well deserves to be
taken seriously, not only by the literary scholar, but by the social
historian and the folklorist.

"The family of the Rackrents," says Thady, "is, I am proud to
say, one of the most ancient in the kingdom — Everybody knows
this is not the old family name, which was O'Shaughlin, related to
the Kings of Ireland" (8-9). The reference here seems to be to the
name of the famous High King of Ireland at the turn of the
eleventh century, Maoilsheachlainn, and we doubtless have an
instance of the folk tendency to assume proof from facile
etymological evidence. What is much more basic to Thady's
attitude, however, is that the Rackrents are seen to derive their
moral authority from their Gaelic ancestry. There is ample
evidence to show that the tests applied by the native Irish in
determining the moral right of landlords were those of nobility of
descent, particularly if it were Gaelic. The objections voiced by
seventeenth-century Gaelic poets to the Cromwellians, for
example, was that these settlers were not of noble ancestry even in
England. An extension of this logic was that highest respect was
due to those nobility who were Gaelic, or had at least some Gaelic

blood, a point which is clear from the works of eighteenth-century Gaelic poets who objected to the Williamite settlers on these criteria. Apart from the social reality of oppression, these attitudes find their basis in the very great importance attributed to genealogy by the Irish from time immemorial. It is also striking that Thady shows that his own ancestors have been servants to the Rackrent family for generations, thus again underlining genealogy as a factor which qualifies social relationships. Because of this, one notices running throughout Thady's narrative, not the servile attitude which the Big House might have expected from a servant, but a feeling of identity and pride which springs from a mutually respected tradition. The strains which the irresponsibility of various members of the Rackrent family put on the relationship account for much of the dramatic tension of the novel, and the eventual destruction of this relationship is heralded by the emergence of the upstart Jason Quirk. Thady's reluctant acceptance of his son's conduct can be explained by his awareness that traditional standards of behaviour no longer hold for either family.

In support of his testimony to the former social distinction of the Rackrents, Thady draws on one famous Irish belief. Before Sir Murtagh Rackrent's death, Thady remarks: "I warned him that I heard the very Banshee that my grandfather heard, before I was born long, under Sir Patrick's window a few days before his death" (16-17). Maria Edgeworth footnotes this in the following way: "The Banshee is a species of aristocratic fairy, who in the shape of a little hideous old woman has been known to appear, and heard to sing in a mournful supernatural voice under the windows of great houses, to warn the family that some of them are soon to die." She then refers to the belief that in the preceding century, "every great family in Ireland had a Banshee." Very few folk beliefs have survived in Ireland with the same tenacity as has that of the banshee. The belief appears to be a purely Gaelic development: the banshee is a female preternatural being whose lamentation is heard announcing the approaching death of a native Irish person, the image being based on that of the ordinary women of this world who keen the dead through the usual "mirror" transmissions of the natural into the extranatural. The intense psychological concentration involved in the communal mind at the crisis time of death provides the functional context for the belief. The banshee is

generally not described very minutely — in fact Maria
Edgeworth's account is probably touched up to some extent; but
the important point here is that the banshee's lamentation is
believed to presage the death of native Irish people only, thus
firmly situating the Rackrents both genealogically and
communally among the native Irish.[1]

The last sentence of this footnote on the banshee is particularly
interesting because the seventeenth century was indeed a
milestone in the development of much of the traditional folklore
surviving into the Ireland of today. There can be little doubt also
that it was in that century that the banshee tradition as we have it
today reached its final development. The Cromwellian plantation
not only shook Irish tradition to its roots, but it also created a new
departure by placing a merchant class in the position of
aristocracy. It is interesting that seventeenth-century references to
the banshee place her in direct opposition to the Cromwellian
planters. Dáibhí Ó Bruadair, the most famous of the century's
poets, mocks the Cromwellians for the cacophony of their names
by comparing them to the — to him — melodious names of famous
otherworld women such as Aoibheall.[2] The nobleman-poet Piaras
Feiritéar, in a lament for a Norman-Gaelic nobleman about the
year 1640, writes this (I translate): "In Dingle the melodious crying
was not spared, so that the merchants of the coastland got
frightened. They need not fear for themselves, since banshees do
not lament their sort."[3] Thady Quirk would not be a true Irish
countryman unless he believed in the fairies. Although there is but
one reference to them in the main body of the text of the novel
(concerning Sir Murtagh who "dug up a fairy-mount against my
advice, and had no luck afterwards" 16), Maria Edgeworth adds a
lengthy footnote here, and appends a long description of the fairy
faith in her Glossary. The belief that misfortune or even death will
befall a person who digs up or defaces a mound or rath believed to
be a fairy abode is familiar all over Ireland, and examples can still
be found today of public authority employees who refuse to
interfere with such objects even when instructed to do so.[4]

It was commonly believed that the fairies travelled in a
whirlwind, an idea probably born of a folk etymology of the Irish
term for the phenomenon *"sí gaoithe"*. The word *sí* here means
"thrust" and has a different derivation from the *sí* designating
mound or mound-dwellers. The folk made such a connection,

however, and thus *sí gaoithe* (meaning "thrust-wind") was taken to be *sí gaoithe* ("wind-fairy") or perhaps more appropriately *sí-ghaoith* ("fairy wind"). Maria Edgeworth refers in her Glossary quite accurately to the custom of saying "God speed ye," or words to that effect, when such a whirlwind rose (106). The purpose of this was to protect people from the dangers of being struck by the fairies, and such a belief is still quite strong in Ireland. Similarly (as Maria Edgeworth rightly states), the fairies are called *the good people* not out of respect or affection; rather is attention deflected from the feelings of fear. *The good people* is simply one of the most common of many euphemistic or flattering terms for the fairies, including "the gentry," "the people of the hills," "the mysterious people" (i.e. *an slua aerach*), "the wee folk," and "the little people."

The Glossary refers to a couple of popular legends about the fairies. Here Maria Edgeworth claims to have heard of these from "an elderly man" (105). It is obvious that she had made an effort to reproduce faithfully the style and words of her informant. Thus she uses, and glosses, dialect words and expressions such as *air and easy* (quietly), *beast* (horse), *lit* (alighted), *mind* (recollect or know), and *mote* (barrow). The first legend concerns a man who was coming back from a fair late at night. He met a man in the dark who invited him to his house, a fine place, where he received food and drink. He fell asleep, but in the morning he found himself lying not in bed but in the angle of the road where he had first met the strange man. "And I asked him what he thought of it, and from first to last he could think of nothing but for certain sure it must have been the fairies that entertained him so well. For there was no house to see any where nigh hand, or any building, or barn, or place at all, but only the church and the *mote* (barrow)" (105-06). There is no doubt here that what we are dealing with is a migratory legend which can be traced quite far back. It is well known, for instance, in Scandinavia and Germany, and is found in Scandinavian medieval literary sources. Saxo Grammaticus records it in his *Gesta Danorum* (c. 1200).[5] Versions of it have been collected in Irish folklore in the last two centuries, notably that published by Patrick Kennedy in his *Legendary Fictions of the Irish Celts* (1866).[6] Similar legends of people brought into the other-world dwellings were very popular in Ireland and can be traced to late mediaeval tradition on the Continent.[7] It is to Maria Edgeworth's credit that this is the earliest known recorded version of this particular legend in Ireland. And an accurate piece of collecting it seems to be.

In the same note Maria Edgeworth recounts another story associated with the fairies. She tells of how corpses that "had not a right to be buried in (a certain) church-yard" could not be interred there, because as the funeral procession would try to enter, everybody's feet would seem to be going backwards instead of forwards. It is evident from Irish folklore generally that people attached tremendous importance to their communal graveyard. Since it is so important for people to rest in their own graveyard, it is understandable that a hostility to the burial of strangers there should arise. One story from County Louth, for example, tells of a man who fell asleep and dreamt that he met three men with a coffin. They made him help them carry it to a graveyard, but they were not allowed to go in because nobody with the same family name as the corpse was resting there. This is repeated in the case of other graveyards, until eventually they come to one where the dead man's family is resting. The three coffin-bearers then release the man from his duties, and he wakes up in the same place as he had fallen asleep.[8] Therefore, though we have as yet found no exact parallel from oral tradition to the story of Maria Edgeworth's informant, there is hardly any doubt but that what she has put before us is a piece of genuine folklore.

Maria Edgeworth also describes one custom of lamenting the dead, which is known in many other civilizations, but was especially strong in Irish tradition up to the last century. Thady's description of Sir Patrick's funeral includes the observation: "Then such a fine whillaluh! You might have heard it to the farthest end of the county, and happy the man who could get but a sight of the hearse!" (11). In her Glossary note on this passage, Maria Edgeworth indicates that the source of her information on the custom of keening the dead lies in the *Transcriptions of the Royal Irish Academy*, but from the details she supplies to Thady's account, it is clear that she also witnessed the custom herself. Three types of lamentation of the dead would have been current in eighteenth-century Gaelic Ireland. First, the spontaneous lamenting of the immediate family and close associates of the dead person. Second, a conventional type of verse-lament, with improvisation, to suit the context, voiced by semi-professional women keeners. Thirdly, a poetic lament composed in strict metre by a literary man for the dead if such were a person of note. The first two types match Maria Edgeworth's description. In the second half of the eighteenth century, a large proportion of the inhabitants of County Longford were still Irish-speaking, and the custom of keening in all its types was closely associated with the use of the native language and did not survive long in English.

Maria Edgeworth has a good deal to say about death-customs apart from keening, and the details she gives here are accurate. Indeed, her notes comprise a valuable contribution to a study of the custom of waking the dead. Wakes as gay social functions, with merriment and games, consumption of tobacco and drink, were until recently, very much part of the Irish way of life. The only suspensions of the rule of liberty would be in the case of the death of a young person, a death in tragic circumstances, or some other public loss, with an exceptional degree of shock or sorrow. The Irish wake tradition may have its roots in ritual placating the dead person and assuring him/her that the living still rejoiced in his/her company.[9] The grotesque account of how Sir Condy pretended to be dead so that he could witness his own funeral can be paralleled by many joke-stories and pranks associated with wakes, such as the tricksters taking the place of the corpse and propping it up so as to make it move. Another parallel is offered by the popular legend of the man who pretended to be dead so as to test his faithless wife (the basis of John Millington Synge's *The Shadow of the Glen*).

In this connection, Sir Condy's trick to secure voting rights for his supporters is of some interest: "Some of our friends were dumbfounded, by the lawyers asking them — had they ever been upon the ground where their freeholds lay? — Now Sir Condy being tender of the consciences of them that had not been on the ground, and so could not swear to a freehold when cross-examined by them lawyers, sent out for a couple of cleaves-full of the sods of his farm of Gulteeshinnagh: and as soon as the sods came into town he set each man upon his sod, and so then ever after, you know, they could fairly swear they had been upon the ground — We gained the day by his piece of honesty" (56). This anecdote is a version of an international folktale, listed as Type No. 1590 in the Aarne-Thompson index, where it is thus summarized: "With earth from his own property in his shoes, the man swears when he is on his neighbour's land, that he is on his own."[10] The footnote report that "This was actually done at an election in Ireland," shows that

Maria Edgeworth had heard it herself. The folktale is known throughout much of Europe, but this is one of the earliest examples of it recorded in Ireland, a fact which puts Irish folklorists in debt to the author of *Castle Rackrent*.[11] In her second edition of the Glossary in 1810, she quotes two other stories of like type from Ireland concerning trick-swearing (124). Both seem to be offshoots from the Irish version of the same international folktale. By thus quoting parallels to her material, Maria Edgeworth shows herself to be following procedures of which a modern folklorist would approve. It is clear that she approaches these materials with honesty and a fair amount of objectivity.

Besides these, the novel exhibits a miscellany of folkways. The author's first Glossary note informs us that it is not by chance that Thady starts his memoirs on a Monday. We are referred to the belief that "no great undertaking can be auspiciously commenced in Ireland on any morning but *Monday morning*," and a number of sayings are quoted in support of the point. The selection of Monday is open to various interpretations. But most simply, as the first workday in the week, the folk mind endows it with special superstitious moment. Since these superstitions have ambivalent implications, we find that side by side with the belief in Monday as a lucky day to undertake some occupation, the belief that Monday is ill-fated. It is not considered lucky, for instance, to shave, to slaughter animals, or to dig a grave on a Monday. It is clear, however, that the positive attitude to Monday prevailed among Maria Edgeworth's sources.

In conclusion, a word about Maria Edgeworth's claim that the culture of *Castle Rackrent* is a thing of the past, a claim which is documented by many explicit details. For instance, the usage "childer" receives the note: "this is the manner in which many of Thady's rank, and others in Ireland, *formerly* pronounced the word *children*" (18n.). Again, a subsequent note states that "It *was* the custom in Ireland for those who could not write, to make a cross to stand for their signature" (45n.). Regarding field forts, her Glossary reports that "*Some years ago,* the common people believed that these Barrows were inhabited by fairies" (105); and further, that "The country people in Ireland certainly *had* great admiration mixed with reverence, if not dread of fairies" (106). Again, referring to banshees, she notes that "latterly their visits and songs have been discontinued" (17n.). We know very well from modern Irish folk tradition that all these statements are false, and that each of these phenomena is very much alive in Ireland today. Why, then does she mislead her readers? We can essay an explanation of this if we consider how she makes the same claim in the more politically sensitive areas of the conduct of the gentry. Colonel M'Guire's mistreatment of his wife (29-30n.) and the various misdeeds of the Rackrents, we are assured, are "no more to be met with at present in Ireland, than Squire Western or Parson Trulliber in England" (Preface, 5). This claim that "the manners depicted ... are not those of the present age" is advanced as an illustration of the social and political observation that "Nations as well as individuals gradually lose attachment to their identity" (5). When we consider that during the writing of *Castle Rackrent*, the great political event of the times, the passage of the Act of Union, constitutionally dissolved Ireland's identity, and that Richard Lovell Edgeworth, M.P. favoured the Act, we can perhaps understand something of his daughter's motives.[12] Was it the emotional conflict engendered by such issues that caused her to shift the action of *Castle Rackrent* to times past? It is clear that *Castle Rackrent* is written "for the information of the *ignorant* English reader" (Preface 4), and the distancing of the action seems to have come from a conflict between her affection for the "other times," despite their shortcomings, and the new — and promising — world opening up with the Union. Maria Edgeworth wishes to be loyal to both the former "Irish Nation," and the newly defined United Kingdom of Great Britain and Ireland. The folklorist can rejoice, however, that she kept her colonial sentiments in abeyance and did not allow them to disfigure the oral material she so skilfully presents in *Castle Rackrent*.

IRISH BULLS IN CASTLE RACKRENT

Cóilín Owens

Castle Rackrent is a work in the ironic mode: its cool, controlled humour runs from dark to black. It is hard to mistake much of it for sentimentality, even Thady Quirk's protestations of "loyalty to the family." Nevertheless, many readers have considered Thady as an uncritical servant of social and economic orders. But Maria Edgeworth's personal contact with Irish country people did not leave her with any misapprehensions about the naiveté of members of his class, skilled as they were in the cultivation of a servility appropriate to their status as minions of a colonial order. She notes that "the lower Irish are such acute observers, that there is no deceiving them as to the state of the real feelings of their superiors. They know the signs of what passes within, more perfectly than any physiognomist, who ever studied the human face, or human head."[1]

The art of *Castle Rackrent*, then, is assuredly complex: it allows the reader the latitude to judge the proportions of calculation, feeling, and self-deception distributed through Thady's account. Certainly *Castle Rackrent* conceals much of what its author knew of the aspirations, resentments, and values of Thady's class in eighteenth-century Ireland. The family papers for the period relevant to the action of *Castle Rackrent* (preserved in the National Library of Ireland: MSS 7361-7362) bear constant reports of agrarian discontent and the activities of Raparees, yet Thady's manner betrays nothing of a tension surely germane to a novel of social and economic relations. Again, Edgeworthstown House was itself threatened by the 1798 Rebellion, and Maria Edgeworth herself visited Ballinamuck immediately after the carnage there: all of this before she submitted the MS of *Castle Rackrent* to her London publisher.

The extensive footnotes and glossary supplied with *Castle Rackrent* indicate Maria Edgeworth's concern that her English readers learn something of native Ireland. And her next literary undertaking, in collaboration with her father, *An Essay on Irish Bulls* (1802), enlarges the defence, drawing it somehwat closer to the substance of the novel.[2] Indeed, Thady Quirk's speech in *Castle Rackrent* exhibits a score of examples of the Irish bull so assiduously dissected in *An Essay*. *An Essay* comprises an extended argument protesting the popular misunderstanding among the English that the Irish are particularly prone to misapprehensions, illogicalities, and solecisms. The Edgeworths respond that this reputation is due to the visitors' mistaking the generosity and good humour of the people and "their habits of using figurative and witty language" for deficiencies of intelligence (300). It is my proposition here that the relationship between *Castle Rackrent* and *An Essay* is more substantial: that the Irish Bull — a general term for a variety of rhetorical tropes in which sense is cunningly encased in apparent nonsense — is a paradigm for the entire novel. Thady's persistence in protesting his loyalty to his masters and his apparent uninterest in his son's usurpation of their former position are a mask for his complicity in these developments and comprise the presiding irony in the novel and supply a coherence we associate with works of the modern period.

For many centuries, indeed for a couple of millenia, Ireland has had a strong tradition in storytelling, speechmaking, debate, and the art of conversation. Just as the ancient tales recount marathon arguments, eloquent boastings, and colourful litanies of curses, so in modern times, visitors to Ireland report — usually with a degree of exaggeration — on the great amount of energy, time, and imagination the Irish invest in talk. The Irish profess to admire most those who can hold their own in any argument, who can "turn a phrase," handle hecklers at a public meeting, or generate what Hugh Kenner has termed "Irish facts."[3] Merited or not, the image prevails in foreign parts that the Irish have "the gift of the gab."

However, it was not always so.

In 1690, for example, a giltedged and leatherbound book appeared in London bearing the title, *Teagueland Jests or Bogg-Witticisms:* "Never before in Print. Published for the Entertainment of all those who are dispos'd to be merry." The title page indicates its two parts: "*The First,* Being a Complete Collection of the Most Learned Bulls, Elaborate Quibbles, and Wise Sayings of some of the Natives of Teagueland, till the year 1688. *The Second* Contains many Comical Stories, and famous Blunders of those Dear Joys, since the late King James's landing amongst them."[4] The anonymous collector then provides a large number of stories of blundering servants and "Comical Joques, called Bulls that are a preposterous kind of speaking." He goes on to explain to his gentle readers that these blunders arise in part "from the great Confusion and Disorder the Irish have been of late," but mainly from "the natural Stupidity and Simplicity of the People; for they [the Blunders] do not appear like little Contrivances, but purely the Effects of the Notions, and Mistakes of Things." This is how the collector relates one of these "Irish bulls" rendered in conventional dialect:

> Another Son of Teagueland drinking Brandy with his Comrade (said to the other) Dear Joy, we mustht not drink too mush Braundy, it will mauke us sleep, and we shall be dead, as mee Friend wash do oder day. Says the other, How dead! He replies, Bee Chreesht I had a dear Friend did drink so mush Brandy he did fall ashleep, and bee Chreesht when he awakened he was dead, yesh indeed (35).

The English attitude towards the witty and humorous speech of the half-Anglicized Irishman has been condescending at best; at worst, it had advanced the prejudice that the native Irish are witty only by accident. But most commentators, such as this Williamite editor, admit a revealing doubt as to whether such "Irish bulls" are the "Effects of their Notions and Mistakes of Things," or are indeed, "Little Contrivances."

English accounts of Ireland since Spenser's time feature the Irishman's proclivity to blunder in speech and action. The anonymous authors of the late seventeenth-century plays, *The Royal Flight* and *The Royal Voyage,* supply a wide range of verbal ineptitude as one of the tags identifying the Stage Irishman. On the eighteenth-century stage — in the works of Sir Robert Howard, John O'Keefe, George Farquhar, the Sheridans and the Colmans — the Irish figures share the same common denominator implied in the name "Teague O'Blunder."

But contrary to the impression left by this caricature, the "Irish bull" is strictly an imported strain. Its first issues appearing in the work cited above. The *Oxford English Dictionary,* having dismissed the alleged connection of the noun "bull" with "a contemptuous allusion to a papal edict," or to a certain Obadiah Bull, suggests an etymology in the Old French *boul, boule, bole* (fraud, deceit, trickery), making its way into the Middle English "bull" (falsehood), and thence into seventeenth-century usage, signifying "a ludicrous jest." However, by the end of that century, this denotation had yielded to the one that concerns us here: "A self-contradictory proposition; in modern usage an expression containing a manifest contradiction in terms, or involving a ludicrous inconsistency unperceived by the speaker. Now often with the epithet *Irish.*" The *Oxford English Dictionary* further notes that "the word had been long in use before it came to be associated with Irishmen," and goes on to list examples from English literary sources in this sense from 1640 into the nineteenth century.

Nevertheless, it has had a particular historical association with supposed errors in the English language made by Irishmen. In this respect, the ascription derives from the Englishman's complacent attitude towards the native Irish, which as Vivian Mercier observes, persists to our own day.[5] One historical figure who may have contributed significantly to the growth of this stereotype was Sir Boyle Roche, Viscount Fermoy (1743-1807), the soldier, MP, and master of ceremonies at Dublin Castle. His speeches in the Irish House of Commons were littered with carcasses such as these: in arguing for the Union, "he would have the two sisters [England and Ireland] embrace like one brother"; and proposing the Habeas Corpus Suspension Bill in Ireland, "it would surely be better, Mr Speaker, to give up not only a *part,* but, if necessary, even the *whole,* of our constitution, to preserve the *remainder!*"[6] But as Sir Jonah Barrington remarks, Sir Boyle Roche's bulls "were rather logical perversions, and had some strong point in most of them."[7] This is confirmed by the discovery among Roche's papers of the notes which were used to weave these "unconventional" bulls into his speeches.

The unease of many commentators about how dull an Irishman may be when he commits a "bull" is, therefore, well advised. Coleridge's definition, that a bull "consists in a mental juxtaposition of incongruous ideas with the sensation, but without the sense of connection," does not apply to the "bulls" of Sir Boyle Roche. They are variations on the ancient rhetorical device of *catachresis:* the deliberate straining of a word or phrase for rhetorical effect, or the borrowing of terms contrary to the idea which is meant to be expressed. The particularly Irish dimension to the "Irish bull" is the retention of the appearance of ignorance, philistinism, or servility, as the instance demands.

It is in this historical context that the Edgeworths saw the necessity for their *Essay.* It is a heavyhanded and pedantic assault on the English prejudice towards Irish speech, drawing ponderously on classical references, doubtful glosses and etymologies, as it lumbers along in an ill-fitting syllogistic greatcoat. But it demonstrates its authors' relative liberality of judgment, their certain degree of familiarity with the Irish countryman, and most remarkable zeal in arguing their case. The argument runs thus: "if we attempt to judge the genius of the lower classes of the people, whether in Ireland or England, we must take care, that we are not under the influence of any prejudice of an aristocratic or literary nature" (164-65); blunders in speech are found internationally (213); many Irish blunders are in fact parallel to or extracted from foreign antecedents (29 *ff.*); it must be borne in mind that Irish is Ireland's native language (7-8), which partly excuses "the great and shameful defect" of the Irish brogue (198); it often takes fine critical sense to distinguish genuine wit from blunder, especially in unfamiliar dialect (113, 190); "the Irish nation, from the highest to the lowest, in daily conversation about the ordinary affairs of life, employ a superfluity of wit, metaphor, and ingenuity which would be astonishing and unintelligible to a majority of the respectable body of English yeomen. Even the cutters of corn and drawers of whisky are orators: even the *cottiers* and *gossoons* speak in trope and figure" (161); Irish wits are disposed to sophistry, and acuteness expresses itself in the arts of deception and chicanery (185). Hence the authors feel obliged to protest that the persistent caricature of the Irish as blundering misusers of language is drawn from ignorance of native genius (301) or race prejudice (280-81). The Edgeworths cite a rich lode of examples supporting these positions, and conclude that Englishmen confuse their own bulls with the Irishman's native crossbreed of ellipsis, catachresis, sophistry, and oxymoron, showing but the motley of stage Irishry.

In their epilogue to the *Essay,* the authors point to the warm reception "a late publication" received in Ireland as evidence of the soundness of their argument. That "late publication" was none other than Maria Edgeworth's own *Castle Rackrent,* which had appeared in three editions in 1800 and 1801. The authors of *An Essay* explain that the good reception of *Castle Rackrent* among their peers was due to Irish landlords' ability "to laugh at the caricature of their ancient foibles" (301). The characterization of the conduct of Irish landlords as "ancient foibles" eighty years before the Land League strikes a modern reader as more than a trifle self-serving.[8] But the more germane point here is how calculated we find the caricature of Thady Quirk, the narrator of *Castle Rackrent.*

Although the character of Thady is in outline drawn according to the conventions of the stage Irishman, in substance he is a skilled survivor in the struggle between landlord and peasant in late eighteenth-century Ireland. And among the devices he so adroitly manages, is the presentation of self as a loyal, honest, deferential, and fawning servant, the finest specimen of peasant on the premises of Castle Rackrent. But much of this is conscious or unconscious deception of self, masters, or readers: for although his image appears to fade along with the family's, it is clear that in the end his son inherits the property, as Thady laconically notes. We may explain Thady's apparently disdainful handling of such an event by reference to his awareness that his readers are English. Thus, just as his actions are in part designing, manipulative, and cunning, so is his account of them finely calculated to exclude all but his most perceptive readers from the realization of the complexity of his motives. His speech expresses an apparently plodding deference in one direction, but implies an acute self-interest in another. His speech is studded with examples of the "Irish bull"; some scenes dramatize such a locution, and indeed the "Irish bull" is arguably a paradigm for the whole manner of the telling of the Rackrent family saga.

First, in the character of Thady Quirk, Maria Edgeworth draws on two of the eight or ten types of the literary convention of the stage Irishman current in 1800: the Fortune Hunter and the Serving Man. The feat of the novel is the author's manipulation of the narrative so that while Thady appears to be one (Servant), he is actually another (Fortune Hunter).[9] Much of the critical discussion of *Castle Rackrent* has centered on how knowing Thady actually is throughout the story; and assessments run the gamut from the naive to the utterly malign. There can be little argument, however, that if Thady doesn't consciously collude with his son, he at the very least acquiesces in the dispossession of his former masters.

Secondly, like an "Irish bull," *Castle Rackrent* is an example of the oral arts: Thady's account is permeated by colloquialisms, hesitations and repetitions; and he pauses "for breath" one-third way through (37). As a story told "out of face," it is a remarkable performance of recollection, concentration, exactitude (in the use of legal terms, for example), and humour and a signal compliment to the verbal skills of Maria Edgeworth's source, John Langan.[10] His speech is "peculiar" only to utter strangers such as the Jewish wife of Sir Kit and *Castle Rackrent's* readers — who are provided with an extensive glossary of such locutions as "kilt," "weed ashes," "duty work," and the Irish practices of "wakes," "keening," and deferring work until "Monday morning."

Third, the narrative provides a number of fine examples of the "Irish bull," mainly from Thady's lips: of Sir Murtagh he stoutly boasts that "Out of forty-nine suits which he had, he never lost one but seventeen" (15); Bella, the young ladies agree, "was the happiest bride ever they had seen, and that to be sure a love match was the only things for happiness, where the parties could any way afford it" (52); of Sir Condy, Thady protests, "he ... was very ill used by the government about a place that was promised him and never given, after his supporting them against his conscience very honourably, and being greatly abused for it" (61); and many others, including the last sentence of the novel in which Thady shrugs, "where's the use of telling lies about the things which every body knows as well as I do?" (96). Now, it is difficult to mistake these knowing statements for Irish blundering, either in their own terms, or in their dramatic or narrative contexts, which demonstrate their function as means of facilitating Jason's advantage at the expense of the Rackrents.

Fourth, the narrative includes dramatizations of specific bulls, such as the comic scene in which Sir Condy pursues a "great fancy to see my own funeral afore I die" (81-73)! This effort to overhear his own obituaries is successful, but not reassuring to Sir Condy, who in his consternation almost betrays his ruse. This leads Thady to advise: "God bless you, and lie still quiet ... a bit longer, for my shister's afraid of ghosts, and would die on the spot with the fright, was she to see you come to life all on a sudden this way without the least preparation" (82): a bull within a bull! Another dramatization of an Irish bull can be found in Lady Rackrent's road accident and its sequel, when she "that was is kilt and lying for dead" (84) survives to pursue litigation — the surest sign of life (96)!

Finally, in the dissembling patter of Thady, his apparent gaffes throughout the story, his protestations of constant concern for the good name of the family, his dubious advice to his succession of masters, his suspension of a revealing detail until a scene has run its apparent course, we recognize the attempt to distract our attention from what is really going on. The persona that Thady holds before the "Quality" is meant for us too, and we are persuaded that to a certain extent even Thady sometimes believes in it rather than in his drive for power. However we may read his character, we observe in it a complex combination of parochialism, sentimentality and loquacity on the one hand, and of acuity, cynicism, and ruthlessness on the other: aspects of character analogous to the elements of wit and phrasing that distinguish an "Irish bull" from a mere blunder. *Castle Rackrent* is *An Essay* fictionalized, therefore; or rather (since *Castle Rackrent* appeared first), *An Essay,* in the words of its authors, is a "betrayal" of the high ambitions of that pioneering Anglo-Irish novel into "the language of panegyric" (301-02). Each work foreshadows a radical shift in the sympathies of the literary elite towards the Irish countryman, his values and language, which continues in the works of Carleton, Yeats, Synge and Fitzmaurice.

In this revised Irish countryman, the "Irish bull" becomes revalued. It is a prized feature of much writing about Irish life: an example not of the Irishman's incapacity for clear and incisive thinking, but of his penchant for wordplay, the exposure of cliché, or logical jest. A few recent examples: "Children is the curse of this country, especially if you haven't any" (reported by Conrad Arensberg); "Irish drama is not what it used to be, and never was" (Lennox Robinson); "I'll live if it kills me" (Flann O Brien); "One man is as good as another, and maybe a damn sight better" (overheard at a local election); "Sure I could play that myself if I knew how" (overheard at a fiddling contest); "Wagner's operas are really much better than they sound" (Shaw). Teagueland jests have evolved into respectable, treasured witticisms.

Thus from a comparison of the intention and argument of *An Essay* and *Castle Rackrent*, we can conclude that like Mahaffey's Irish bull "that is always pregnant," Thady's "poor" qualities exhibit representative Irish humour, political and linguistic skills, and are not mere quirks of individual character.

CASTLE RACKRENT: **THE DISINGENUOUS THADY QUIRK**[1]

James Newcomer

That fortune is not nice in her morality, that she frequently
favours those who do not adhere to truth more than those who
do, we have early had occasion to observe.

Maria Edgeworth, *Helen* (X, 350)

Since the publication of Maria Edgeworth's *Castle Rackrent* in 1800
there has been a consensus of the critics concerning the character of
the narrator, Thady Quirk. The more perceptive have pointed to
the curiously enigmatic quality of the story and Thady's
contribution to that quality. But in the main the critics have been
content to refer to him as "the old family retainer," characterized
by an unthinking and prejudiced loyalty. They pay tribute to Miss
Edgeworth for creating him, but there is doubt that anyone yet has
perceived exactly the kind of man that Thady is. The originality of
Castle Rackrent and its influence on subsequent novelists being what
they were, it is a matter of importance to understand correctly the
qualities of the central character in the novel.

We should at the least be sceptical of the ingenuousness and the
loyalty that appear to be Thady's characteristics. If he is simple, he
has the native shrewdness that may sometimes be the companion
of simplicity; if he is loyal to the family, that loyalty is made
somewhat more comfortable by the perquisities that have
accompanied his service. It is in the character of his crafty,
grasping son Jason, who by the end of the novel is master of the
Rackrent estate, that we see reflected, as in an imperfect mirror,
the projection of Thady's simplicity and faithfulness; and of course
in the reflection the simplicity has become sophistication and the
faithfulness, self-serving.

If this judgement is correct, it contradicts the critics from
Lawless to Flanagan. Jeffares, when he says that "the art of Maria
disappears in the artlessness of Thady, and, one might add, the
artfulness of his son Jason,"[2] makes her imagination as it appears in
these two characters a simple contrast between black and white.
Gerould, when he says that "Thady Quirk, an old family retainer,
was made to tell in his own simple-minded and confused way how

the Rackrent family came to ruin,"[3] reduces Thady's shrewd simplicity to mere simple-mindedness; and, incidentally, this observation reduces Miss Edgeworth's art to artfulness. Flanagan, who is more perceptive on the subject of the Edgeworth novels than others (perhaps because he has a deeper knowledge of the Irish), finds that "the acts and statements are ambiguous and unsettling,"[4] but this observation turns out to be only a near miss when he speaks of "the disparity between the family as it exists in fact and as it appears to the imagination of the peasant Thady."[5]

For Thady is ever and always the realist. How does he begin his story? Not with "I and mine have lived time out of mind" but with "I and mine have lived rent free time out of mind" (7) upon the Rackrent estate. How innocent of judgement is he when he says what follows of Sir Murtagh's lady?

> However, my lady was very charitable in her own way. She had a charity school for poor children, where they were taught to read and write gratis, and where they were kept well to spinning gratis for my lady in return . . . (13).

Since there is no evidence that he was not on good terms with all the servants and the tenantry, we are not to suppose that when he pays tribute to Lady Rackrent's husbandry he is not also exposing, deliberately, her parsimony. So great is the burden that Sir Murtagh and his wife laid on the tenants that they were "always breaking and running away" (14), and from Thady's summary of their afflictions we wonder that they had even a morsel for themselves after providing the bounty that the landlords consumed. Thady, who is one of the peasantry, could not in all reason witness the suffering that came from affliction and present that affliction in such revealing detail without meaning to render judgment. We find a clue to this conclusion a few pages later when Thady is writing about the heir, Sir Kit:

> Bad news still for the poor tenants, no change still for the better with them — Sir Kit Stopgap my young master, left all to the agent, and though he had the spirit of a Prince, and lived away to the honour of his country abroad, which I was proud to hear of, what were we the better for that at home (20)?

Here his sympathy and his criticism are both plain. And though he spreads a shadow of defence across the picture of suffering that he paints, and his voice has the tone of the sycophant, his indictment is plain and sincere:

> The agent was one of your middle men, who grind the face of the poor, and can never bear a man with a hat upon his head — he ferreted the tenants out of their lives — not a week without a call for money — drafts upon drafts from Sir Kit — but I laid it all to the fault of the agent; for, says I, what can Sir Kit do with so much cash, and he a single man (20-21)?

Certainly this is all disingenuous.

What are the loyalties of the man who tells us that when Sir Kit came home with his bride "I held the flam full in her face to light her, at which she shuts her eyes, but I had a full view of the rest of her, and greatly shocked I was" (24-25)? And how self-deluded is the man who tells us that

> there were now no less than three ladies in our county talked of for his second wife, all at daggers drawing with each other, as his gentleman swore, at the balls, for Sir Kit for their partner — I could not but think them bewitched, but they all reasoned with themselves, that Sir Kit would make a good husband to any Christian, but a Jewish, I suppose, and especially as he was now a reformed rake; and it was not known how my lady's fortune was settled in her will, nor how the Castle Rackrent estate was all mortgaged, and bonds out against him, for he was never cured of his gaming tricks — but that was the only fault he had, God bless him (32)!

That certainly is not simple-minded, or self-deluded, or ingenuous.

The evidence of Thady's clear-headed judgment continues to reveal itself in the section dealing with Sir Kit's wife:

> All these civilities wrought little with my lady, for she had taken an unaccountable prejudice against the country and every thing belonging to it ... (35-36). [She had been immured in her room only seven years by her husband!]
>
> Had she meant to make any stay in Ireland, I stood a great chance of being a great favourite with her, for when she found I understood the weather-cock, she was always finding some pretence to be talking to me, and asking me which way the wind blew, and was it likely, did I think, to continue fair for England

(36). [Thady knows which way the wind blows.]

This much I thought it lay upon my conscience to say, in justice to my poor master's memory (36). [How black a character his conscience has given his master!]

The calculating mind of Thady shows itself in relation to two other characters particularly — in the affair of his niece Judy to a rather slight extent, and to a great degree in the role that his son Jason plays. Judy loses the opportunity to become the wife of Sir Condy, but not before her great-uncle Thady has made a final ploy to help her. It appears that Sir Condy will choose Isabella Moneygawl; but when he is in his cups, he decides, at Thady's suggestion, to flip a coin to make his choice between the two girls. It is not Thady's fault that the gamble fails to pay off by advancing a Quirk to the position of mistress of the estate.

Thady is successful, though, through Jason. It is evident that his fine finger helps manipulate Jason's rise to affluence and power. In no other connection do Thady's actions so much belie the easy conception of him as the ignorant, faithful retainer. Thady may not have planned that Jason displace the Rackrents, but the groundwork that Thady lays makes it possible for Jason to seize the opportunities that come his way. The evidence of Thady's astuteness lies largely concealed, but breaks through not once or twice, merely, but time and again — often enough and subtly enough to prove both the author's intentions and her subtle artistry.

"I wash my hands of his doings," says Thady of his son Jason on page eight, "and as I have lived so will I die, true and loyal to the family." But this is in keeping with his relationship with Jason throughout the story, and it confirms his loyalty to the Rackrents not at all. Except in Jason's first moves, Thady appears to play no part — apparently he has washed his hands long since — but there is evidence that Jason is acting not out of sympathy with his father.

The expressions "my son" and "my son Jason" occur no fewer than thirty times in the short novel. Not only does the frequency attract attention, but also the situations in which Thady emphasizes his relationship with Jason. How is it, but through Thady, that Jason gets the opportunity to serve the estate agent as clerk? When Jason puts in for the possession of a valuable lease, "I spoke a good word for my son," Thady says, "and gave out in the country, that nobody need bid against us" (22). Note the word *us* — inadvertent on Thady's part if we could keep him in character, but surely deliberate on the part of Miss Edgeworth. When the agent is turned out, "my son Jason, who had corresponded privately with his honor occasionally on business, was forthwith desired by his honor to take the accounts into his own hands . . . ." (23) Privately? How is it that Thady has been privy to that correspondence?

When Thady apologizes to Sir Kit's new wife for the few bonfires that have greeted her, "Jason and I forbid them" (25), he says. When Sir Kit dies, Thady tells us that *"We* got the key out of his pocket the first thing *we* did, and my son Jason ran to unlock the barrack-room, where my lady had been shut up for seven years, to acquaint her with the fatal accident" (33). [Italics added, Ed.]

One would suppose, if Thady is as loyal to the family and as disapproving of Jason as he declares himself to be, that he would not emphasize the father-son relationship, especially in those instances when Jason is marking off the steps toward the Rackrents' ruin. But it is precisely in those instances that Thady speaks of "my son Jason." We have already seen that Thady has been an instrumentality in his son's early affluence. The following quotations reveal Thady's identification with Jason in his continuing rise in the world. It is "my son Jason" who makes Sir Condy see how financially distressed he is; it is "my son" who requires to be paid for his "many years service in the family gratis" (41); it is "my son" who receives a lease from Sir Condy at a bargain and makes "two hundred a year profit rent, which was little enough, considering his long agency" (41). It is a hunting lodge near "my son Jason's land" that Jason hopes to acquire from Sir Condy.

When the bills come in thick and fast, "my son Jason had 'em all handed over to him, and the pressing letters were all unread by Sir Condy, who hated trouble . . ." (52). When the Rackrents are so poor that at a company dinner they run out of candles, it is "to my son Jason's" that they send to borrow some. At this point, "my son Jason put in a word again about the lodge," and "it was a good bargain for both parties, for my son bought the fee simple of a good house for him and his heirs for ever for little or nothing, and by selling of it for that same my master saved himself from a gaol" (54).

Up to this last event matters may be working out for Jason and the Rackrents as Thady wishes them to. He is pleased enough with Jason's rise in the world, and Sir Condy's election to Parliament provides the Rackrents with a new lease on life. But this nice balance is not long maintained, and it is Thady himself who in his next move seals Sir Condy's fate. It is evident up to this point that Thady had deliberately helped his son to affluence at the Rackrents' expense. Whether his next move is deliberate or not (it is impossible to be positive here), certain it is that Thady finds the man and delivers the information that together destroy the Rackrents. Ironically, Thady sets in motion the machinery that finishes off the Rackrents at the very moment of Sir Condy's triumph, his election to Parliament.

The scene is a public house at the height of the election drinking. The stranger says:

". . . there was a great report of his being ruined." "No matter," says I [Thady], "the sheriffs two years running were his particular friends, and the sub-sheriffs were both of them gentlemen, and were properly spoken to; and so the writs lay snug with them, and they, as I understand by my son Jason the custom in them cases is, returned the writs as they came to them to those that sent 'em; much good may it do them! with a word in Latin, that no such person as Sir Condy Rackrent, Bart., was to be found in those parts." "Oh, I understand all those ways better, no offense, than you," says he, laughing, and at the same time filling his glass to my master's good health, which convinced me he was a warm friend in his heart after all, though appearances were a little suspicious or so at first. "To be sure," says he, still cutting his joke, "when a man's over head and shoulders in debt, he may live the faster for it, and the better, if he goes the right way about it; or else how is it so many live on so well, as we see every day, after they are ruined?" How is it," says I, being a little merry at the time; "how is it but jut as you see the ducks in the chicken-yard, just after their heads are cut off by the cook, running round and round faster than when alive?" At which conceit he fell a laughing, and remarked he had never had the happiness yet to see the chicken-yard at Castle Rackrent. "It won't be long so, I hope," sais I; "you'll be kindly welcome there, as everybody is made by my master: there is not a freer spoken gentleman, or a better beloved, high or low, in all

Ireland . . . ." And little did I think at the time, or till long after,
how I was harbouring my poor master's greatest of enemies
myself. This fellow had the impudence, after coming to see the
chicken-yard, to get me to introduce him to my son Jason; little
more than the man that never was born did I guess at his
meaning by this visit: he gets him a correct list fairly drawn out
from my son Jason of all my master's debts, and goes straight
round to the creditors and buys them all up" (IV, 36-37).

Thady is playing the part of the opportunist here, his disclaimers
notwithstanding. His eyes are wide open to the imminent
destruction of his master's family, as we know from the realistic and
cynical sentence about the ducks with their heads cut off. Within
the context of the chicken-yard figure, he offers, casually as it were,
the invitation to visit the Castle, and contrives the introduction to
"my son Jason." He has set the juggernaut rolling that will destroy
Sir Condy. Jason will join forces with the visitor, they will bring an
execution against the entire Rackrent property, and what has
belonged to the Rackrents will henceforth belong to the Quirks.

From this point in the story we shall be most nearly honest if we
judge the evidence against Thady to be inconclusive. The chicken-
yard speech is damning, but a sense of humour, mixed motives,
and tipsiness may combine to give flawed evidence. Jason is still
"my son Jason," even if Thady does not share in his son's new
affluence; and Sir Condy is still "my master" even when he has no
land or servants.

A final irony concerning Thady's part in the Rackrents' ruin
derives from the great drinking horn of Sir Condy's forebear, Sir
Patrick. Sir Condy "was fond often of telling the story that he
larned from me when a child, how Sir Patrick drank the full of this
horn without stopping, and this was what no other man afore or
since could without drawing breath" (93-94).

As a result of these stories, Sir Patrick has ever been Sir Condy's
model. Now, with only his life left to him, Sir Condy orders Thady
to fill the horn for him. "And so wishing his honor success, I did
. . . He swallows it down, and drops like one shot" (95). So it is that
Sir Condy meets his death, with Thady at his side to help him to his
dying, as Thady had helped him to his penury.

Faithful Thady! the old family retainer — generations of
readers have taken these words at their face value, pleased with the

character as they think Miss Edgeworth created it, satisfied aesthetically, perceiving no more and asking no more than they perceive. It is something of a measure of her achievement that her novel should have been enjoyed and praised without readers recognising the full dimensions of its central character.

The Thady whom we now recognize is a more important creation than Thady the unreflecting servant. Far from being simple, he is relatively complex. The true Thady reflects intellect and power in the afflicted Irish peasant, who in generations to come will revolt and revolt again. He is artful rather than artless, unsentimental rather than sentimental, shrewd rather than obtuse, clear-headed rather than confused, calculating rather than trusting. There is less affection in our view of the true Thady, but now we have to feel a degree of admiration for him.

Seeing Thady in a new light, we perceive subtleties and complexities that colour the tone and complicate the plot of the novel. Consequently, we recognise Maria Edgeworth now to have been more imaginately creative in *Castle Rackrent* than our old conception of Thady Quirk permitted her to be.

TRANSPARENT THADY QUIRK[1]

Elizabeth Harden

Thady Quirk is the most alive and complete of all Miss Edgeworth's character creations, and one critic has considered him "the most subtly drawn and skilfully presented character in the whole course of the Irish novel."[2] In his efforts to please his masters, his willingness to serve, and his obedience to duty, Thady affirms his unyielding allegiance to the lords of the Rackrent estate and to all that the estate represents. His general attitude toward the family — however great their faults have been — is one of wholesome acceptance; he takes pride in recognizing the Rackrent family as "one of the most ancient in the kingdom." He is honoured to have shared the family heritage, and he feels confident that the world will be as interested in each intimate detail of his narrative as he is.[3] Thady has learned early in life the wisdom of reticence, and because of his discretion he becomes the peacemaker, the friend, and the confidant to the members of the discordant households. "I said nothing, for I had a regard for the family," Thady remarks, or "I put my pipe in my mouth and kept my mind to myself; for I had a great regard for the family." The "family" has become the symbol of a way of life for Thady, and even of the iniquitous Sir Kit, Thady remarks, "I loved him from that day to this, his voice was so like the family" (19).

Thady is poignantly real because Miss Edgeworth understands him completely and exposes both his inner and outer life — his inner life through the transparency of his nature, his outer life through his assertions and external manner. The author is able to identify herself with him completely, to capture the fleeting subtleties of his mind and the psychological motives of his behaviour with remarkable precision. In her last novel, *Helen*, Miss Edgeworth, the teacher, converts the subject of truth into a thesis and urges the explication of the thesis as the primary goal in the novel. In her first novel, *Castle Rackrent*, Miss Edgeworth, the artist, concentrates first on creating a character, and because that character is Thady Quirk — distinct, individual, unlike any other creation — the qualities of truth, sincerity, and sobriety become indispensable requisites to his nature and are all the more appealing because they emanate from the depths of his character. "There's nothing but truth in it from beginning to end," Thady says at the close of his narrative, and his strikingly simple introduction of himself is the first of the many proofs of his assertion:

— My real name is Thady Quirk, though in the family I have always been known by no other than 'honest Thady' — afterwards, in the time of Sir Murtagh, deceased, I remember to hear them call me 'old Thady;' and now I'm come to 'poor Thady' — for I wear a long great coat winter and summer, which is very handy, as I never put my arms into the sleeves, (they are as good as new,) though, come Holantide next, I've had it these seven years; it holds on by a single button round my neck, cloak fashion — to look at me, you would hardly think 'poor Thady' was the father of attorney Quirk; he is a high gentleman, and never minds what poor Thady says, and having better than 1500 a-year, landed estate, looks down upon honest

Thady, but I wash my hands of his doings, and as I have lived so will I die, true and loyal to the family (7-8).

Thady unhesitatingly confesses his personal prejudices; he cannot forgive Sir Murtagh's wife because he suspects that she "had Scotch blood in her veins"; yet he compliments his lady on her charity. He is proud that Sir Kit "lived away to the honour of his country abroad," but he candidly admits that business matters at home fared badly, because his master "was a little too fond of play." He dislikes his new lady, Sir Kit's wife, because she is Jewish: "Mercy upon his honor's poor soul, thought I, what will become of him and his, and all of us, with this heretic Blackamore at the head of the Castle Rackrent estate" But he eases the tension between her and his master by explaining to her the nature and purpose of the trees, planted near the bog of Allyballycarricko'shaughlin. Thady perceives Sir Condy's folly in accepting Isabella Moneygawl rather than Judy M'Quirk as a wife; for the affected, presumptuous Isabella appears to Thady as a "mad woman for certain, which is . . . bad." But he accepts her unquestionably as his master's choice and is thankful that she is not a skinflint like Sir Murtagh's wife.

Thady's "mellow goodness," his freshness, his innocence spring from the uniformity of his temperament and an incomparable disposition to be happy with his lot in life. He would not exchange the contentment of his commonplace existence for the prestige of having been born a gentleman. Yet in his sympathy with human beings more unfortunate than he and in his capacity for pity, in his ability to negate or lose his identity in something larger than himself, he becomes heroic in stature. His sympathetic openness is most apparent in his feelings toward Sir Condy. He reprimands the creditor's agent who would interrupt the rejoicing over Sir Condy's victory in the election: "Put it [a written order for Sir Condy's arrest] in your pocket again, and think no more of it any ways for seven years to come, my honest friend . . . he's a member of Parliament now, praised be God, and such as you can't touch him; and if you'll take a fool's advice, I'd have ye keep out of the way this day, or you"ll run a good chance of getting your deserts amongst my master's friends, unless you chuse to drink his health like every body else" (57). Thady's reverence and admiration for Sir Condy and his duty toward his son create within him an acute psychological conflict when Jason is ready to force Sir Condy off

the estate: "Oh, Jason! Jason! how will you stand to this in the face
of the county, and all who know you, (says I); "and what will
people tink and say, when they see you living here in Castle
Rackrent, and the lawful owner turned out of the seat of his
ancestors, without a cabin to put his head into, or so much as a
potatoe to eat?" (77). Sir Condy must at last pay for the
accumulated doom of the Rackrent generations and sign away the
deed of the estate to Jason; Thady, realizing that his son takes
possession of the estate because of his guile rather than because of
his ability, describes the transaction with suppresed emotion:

> So he signed — and the man who brought in the punch
> witnessed it, for I was not able, but crying like a child; and
> besides, Jason said, which I was glad of, that I was no fit witness,
> being so old and doating. It was so bad with me, I could not taste
> a drop of the punch itself, though my master himself, God bless
> him! in the midst of his trouble, poured out a glass for me and
> brought it up to my lips. — 'Not a drop, I thank your honor's
> honor as much as if I took it though,' and I just set down the glass
> as it was and went out; and when I got to the street door, the
> neighbour's childer who were playing at marbles there, seeing
> me in great trouble, left their play, and gathered about me to
> know what ailed me; and I told them all, for it was a great relief
> to me to speak to these poor childer, that seemed to have some
> natural feeling left in them ... (78).

Thady has the incalculability of life about him, and he is never
more real, never more human than in his moments of loneliness: "I
had nobody to talk to, and if it had not been for my pipe and
tobacco, should, I verily believe, have broke my heart for poor Sir
Murtagh," a bewildered Thady remarks when the household is
topsy-turvy and all is mass confusion with the accession of Sir Kit.
During the winter when Sir Condy is away in Dublin, attending
his duties in Parliament, Thady is left alone at the estate with
boards that creak, hangings that flap, winds that meet little
resistance. His loneliness, which never descends into self-pity,
assumes a universal quality:

> I was very lonely when the whole family was gone, and all the
> things they had ordered to go and forgot sent after them by the
> stage. There was then a great silence in Castle Rackrent, and I
> went moping from room to room, hearing the doors clap for

want of right locks, and the wind through the broken windows that the glazier never would come to mend, and the rain coming through the roof and best ceilings all over the house, for want of the slater whose bill was not paid; besides our having no slates or shingles for that part of the old building which was shingled, and burnt when the chimney took fire, and had been open to the weather ever since. I took myself to the servants' hall in the evening to smoke my pipe as usual, but missed the bit of talk we used to have there sadly, and ever after was content to stay in the kitchen and boil my little potatoes, and put up my bed there; and every post day I looked in the newspaper, but no news of my master in the house. — He never spoke good or bad ... (61).

Thady is the one flawless product of Miss Edgeworth's creative imagination, for she was conscious of a method that directed her in his creation — a method which she adapted so skilfully to her medium that Thady's naive utterances frequently attain an eloquence that is all the more convincing because it is entirely consistent with his character. Miss Edgeworth's lengthiest comment on the composition of *Castle Rackrent* is found in a letter to Mrs Stark, who had sent to Maria Colonel Stewart's long criticism of *Helen*. While the comment is not indicative of any clear-cut literary theory, it does intimate that Miss Edgeworth's effort was highly conscious, but not self-conscious, and it reveals an approach based on the freedom to feel and say — a liberty which Miss Edgeworth never again presumed completely in her writings:

The only character drawn from the life in *Castle Rackrent* is Thady himself, the teller of the story. He was an old steward (not very old, though, at that time; I added to his age, to allow him time for the generations of the family). I heard him when I first came to Ireland, and his dialect struck me, and his character; and I became so acquainted with it, that I could think and speak in it without effort: so that when, for mere amusement, without any idea of publishing, I began to write a family history as Thady would tell it, he seemed to stand beside me and dictate; and I wrote as fast as my pen would go, the characters all imaginary. Of course they must have been compounded of persons I had seen or incidents I had heard; but how compounded I do not know: not by "long forethought," for I had never thought of them till I began to write, and had made no sort of plan, sketch, or framework. There is a fact mentioned in a note, of Lady Cathcart having been shut up by her husband, Mr McGuire, in a house in this neighbourhood. So much I knew, but the characters are totally different from what I had heard. Indeed, the real people had been so long dead, that little was known of them. Mr McGuire had no resemblance, at all events, to my Sir Kit; and I knew nothing of Lady Cathcart but that she was fond of money, and would not give up her diamonds. Sir Condy's history was added two years afterwards: it was not drawn from life, but the good-natured and indolent extravagances were suggested by a relation of mine long since dead. All the incidents pure invention: the duty work and duty fowls, facts . . . .[4]

The critical reader of *Castle Rackrent* wishes that Miss Edgeworth had said more. For Thady's great appeal lies in his simple charm and unconscious naiveté, made possible by the artistic device of "transparency" — the ironic presentation of external fact in such a manner that the reader may see the truth underneath the external statement and draw his own conclusions.[5] Essentially, the events of Thady's narrative may be viewed from a three-dimensional level: the factual level in which the author has selected and arranged the events, typical of the world from which they are taken; the interpretative level of Thady, in which the events are filtered through his understanding; the interpretative level of the reader, who is able to see through and beyond Thady. For example, while the false report of Jessica's death is being circulated and the county speculates on three different ladies for Sir Kit's second wife, Thady remarks:

— I could not but think them bewitched, but they all reasoned with themselves, that Sir Kit would make a good husband to any Christian, but a Jewish, I suppose, and especially as he was now a reformed rake; and it was not known how my lady's fortune was settled in her will, nor how the Castle Rackrent estate all all mortgaged, and bonds out against him, for he was never cured of his gaming tricks — but that was the only fault he had, God bless him (32)!

On the factual level, Sir Kit's being a reformed rake, his insecure financial status, and his weakness for gambling render him a complete rogue and an unfortunate marital prospect for any lady

of consequence. As the statement filters through Thady's understanding, it becomes ironic understatement because of his
complete failure to understand its serious implications. The reader,
while he recognizes the impact of the statement, can at the same
time appreciate Thady's simplicity; the plus or minus x, the
unknown quality of the reader's imagination, makes up the totality
of his conclusion.

Again, in denouncing Jessica for bringing only confusion to the
Rackrent household, Thady proclaims: "Her diamond cross was,
they say, at the bottom of it all; and it was a shame for her, being his
wife, not to show more duty, and to have given it up when he
condescended to ask so often for such a bit of a trifle in his distresses,
especially when he all along made it no secret he married for
money" (36). The assertion obviously unmasks the deceptive
nature of Sir Kit who unsuccessfully used marriage as an
instrument towards his financial salvation, while at the same time
it justifies Jessica in her obstinate refusal to become such an
instrument. But Thady shows no surprise at what would otherwise
seem incredible, and the reader finds pleasure in the recognition of
incongruities while he forms his own opinion.

In *Castle Rackrent*, Thady serves as the novel's centre of vision.
The point of view, then, is that of a minor character who tells the
main characters' story; but Thady also functions as a character
within the narrative and becomes the focal point of the interest and
inspiration of the novel. Since the annals of the Rackrents are cast
in the form of memoirs, with Thady acting as the author and Miss
Edgeworth posing as the editor, the point of view is highly suitable
for the kind of effect which Miss Edgeworth seeks to establish
within this particular framework. The work is designed with no
greater purpose in view than to serve "as a specimen of Irish
manners and characters, which are, perhaps, unknown in
England." But a faithful, realistic portrayal of such manners and
characters could not present an appealing picture — a gentry,
grown apathetic, irresponsible, and degenerate; a peasantry, poor
squalid, and illiterate; an economic and political system grown
hopelessly corrupt.

Chekov has said, "When you depict sad or unlucky people, and
you want to touch your readers' hearts, try to be cold — it gives
their grief a background against which it stands out in greater
relief."[6] By delineating the events in the mirror of Thady's

reflective consciousness, Miss Edgeworth is able to give them the appearance of bold relief and to sustain the illusion of seriousness, of heightened objectivity, which the story requires. Presenting the picture through the mellow mind of Thady also gives it a warm, glowing appeal. The expanse of life in the novel — the history of a family through four generations — is too extensive to be shown in a series of dramatic scenes. The events, then, are Thady's impressions, pictured and summarized by him for the reader.

Generally, the use of a first-person narrator imposes restrictions, both on the writer, who must reflect the world beyond and outside of his narrator, and on the reader, who is limited to the narrator's thoughts, observations, and feelings. But in *Castle Rackrent*, Thady's unique character and the very limitation of his opportunity for observation and interpretation gives unity to the story, since he provides a frame of reference for all of the events. He has had the opportunity of observing or experiencing all that is finally relevant to the story and is the one most capable of reporting the Rackrent history. Since his views are coloured by his own emotional bias, and especially by his misconception of "family honour," the reader may question his ability as the chief interpreter of the events. We have seen, however, that Miss Edgeworth provides a "threefold vision" through Thady's transparency, and he thus becomes a very capable spokesman who powerfully suggests the outlying associations of events and who provides the sufficient balance of comedy and seriousness in the plot. As Sir Walter Scott has observed, "And what would be the most interesting, and affecting, as well as the most comic passages of *Castle Rackrent*, if narrated by one who had a less regard for the family than the immortal Thady, who, while he sees that none of the dynasty which he celebrates were perfectly right, has never been able to puzzle out wherein they were certainly wrong."[7]

The consistency with which Miss Edgeworth sustains the comic effect in an otherwise serious tale is one of her finest achievements. Since she chose to treat the Irish peasant seriously, and since, furthermore, she made an old peasant — crude, alien, superstitious, naive — the hero of her work, she was able to capture the distinct provincial peculiarities which puzzle, attract, and entertain the reader of *Castle Rackrent*. The comedy, then, arises from the nature of Thady's character, from the quaintness of his Irish idiom, from the strange varieties of Irish character in general, whether serious or gay, and from the tone of ironic detachment, which never changes throughout the narrative. Thady frequently prepares the reader for a scene of great sadness or hopelessness, only to neutralize the effect with a change to comedy or even farce. Instead of lingering over the pathos of Sir Patrick's death, Thady hurries on to describe the lavish funeral. Instead of paying his respects to the deceased Sir Murtagh, Thady emphasizes his eagerness to see his mistress depart from the Rackrent household. When Thady has remarked at length on the hopelessness and desolation of Sir Condy's state of affairs, he changes abruptly to Sir Condy's ambition to see his own funeral before he dies. The grimmest scene in the novel is thus followed by the scene of greatest farce . . . .

Since the plan of *Castle Rackrent* called for a first-person narrator, the selection and arrangement of the details must depend upon Thady. On one hand, the method is advantageous, for it gives free sway to Thady's surmises, doubts, musings, and rambling digressions. At the same time, the method imposes few restrictions on the structure of the plot, which is loose and episodic. The four generations of the Rackrents comprise the major episodes of the novel and are connected by the character of the narrator. The plot is more closely unified than the method would seem to permit, however, since Thady's tale is concerned with a single family estate and with four generations of *one* family. The Rackrent estate is the fixed, recurring symbol which helps to impose order, for it is indispensable in revealing character, in expediting the passage of time, and in delineating the remnants of a dying era. Its gradual downfall and deterioration over the years are a result of its mismanagement by the four generations. Consequently, in each instance, the estate is juxtaposed with its owner, whose character is unfolded in his handling of it. Over a period of years, the estate comes to symbolize a specific way of life of a family who have left their marks upon it. It also suggests a movement in time from apparent integration at the beginning to total disintegration at the end — a disintegration which is marked by the dissolution of a family unit and by the collapse of the estate itself. The death of Sir Condy, then, brings to a close the history of a family, of an estate, and of a way of life. The estate constitutes an important thematic element in the novel, for it illuminates the problems of inheritance by tying together the action of the past and present and by pointing always to the future.

The family lineage also provides unity in the plot, since the repetition of similar character traits establishes a continuous pattern; each generation recalls the reader directly to the central interest of the plot — the decay, disintegration, and final extinction of a family over several generations. The similarities of Sir Patrick and Sir Condy, the first and last of the representatives, are especially significant, for they solidify into one mysterious image the "monument of old Irish hospitality."

Castle Rackrent is undeniably the best evidence of Miss Edgeworth's literary merits. It is all of one texture; brisk in movement, lively in interest, filled with humour and pathos, it arouses our compassion and deepens our tolerance and understanding of a bygone age. It seizes a crucial era in the history of a nation and illuminates a world of forgotten customs and beliefs; it presents a direct impression of a people "fighting like devils for conciliation, and hating one another for the love of God."[8]

Castle Rackrent is noticeably free from all the faults which were to mar Miss Edgeworth's later works — heavy didacticism, wearisome repetitions, improbable exaggerations, elementary discussions, forcd catastrophes. The most substantial and remarkable thing about the novel is the richness — the depth, complexity, and subtlety of its implications. It is therefore especially significant that Miss Edgeworth succeeded in giving the most accurate delineation of character and the most convincing expression of her country's problems in a novel which sought only the presentation of a "specimen of manners and characters." And the measure of her success is the difference between two methods — the method of statement and the method of representation. The major argument which runs throughout Henry James' prefaces to his novels is that in art "what is merely stated is not presented, what is not presented is not vivid, what is not vivid is not represented, and what is not represented is not art."[9] Instead of letting her story suggest the moral, Miss Edgeworth too often lets her moral suggest the story. But in *Castle Rackrent* she took a holiday from her duties as moral teacher, and instead of concentrating on teaching a safe and practical moral lesson, she allowed her characters to fulfil their own destinies and relinquished the duty of pointing a moral to the story itself. She made no attempt to explain human nature, but only to illuminate it. Consequently, what gives the work its ever-present air of reality is that rewards and punishments are the logical outcome of the characters' actions. Nothing is forced, nothing is wearisomely contrived, nothing is bound by the restrictions of theory or conscious moral purpose.

It is apparent, then, why Miss Edgeworth's readers from her own generation to the present day have always felt greatest affection for *Castle Rackrent*. On September 27, 1802, Miss Edgeworth wrote to Mrs Mary Sneyd, "My father asked for *Belinda, Bulls,* etc., found they were in good repute — *Castle Rackrent* in better — the others often borrowed, but *Castle Rackrent* often bought."[10] Sir Walter Scott's warm praises of the work are well known. On one occasion he remarked, "If I could but hit Miss Edgeworth's wonderful power of vivifying all her persons and making them live as *beings* in mind, I should not be afraid."[11] In his "Preface" to *Waverley,* he generously expressed his indebtedness to Miss Edgeworth: "It has been my object to describe these persons, not by a caricatured and exaggerated use of the national dialect, but by their habits, manners, and feelings; so as in some distant degree to emulate the admirable Irish portraits drawn by Miss Edgeworth, so different from the "Teagues" and "dear joys," who so long, with the most perfect family resemblance to each other, occupied the drama and the novel."[12] And Anne Thackeray Ritchie praised Miss Edgeworth for a quality which Sir Walter Scott also possessed: "Her own gift, I think, must have been one of perceiving through the minds of others, for realising the value of what they in turn reflected; one is struck again and again by the odd mixture of intuition, and of absolute matter of fact which one finds in her writings."[13]

In *Castle Rackrent,* Miss Edgeworth drew directly from nature; only in *Castle Rackrent* was she a poet, at least in the sense in which Rupert Brooke used the term: "It consists in just looking at people and things in themselves — neither as useful nor moral nor ugly nor anything else; but just as being."

STYLE AND PURPOSE IN MARIA EDGEWORTH'S FICTION[1]

Joanne Altieri

In the latter part of her long life, Maria Edgeworth wrote to her friend Mrs Stark:

> How I wish I could furnish, as Scott has, some of those pictured tales coloured to the life; but I fear I have not that power, therefore it is perhaps that I strive to console myself for my deficiencies of flattering myself that there is much, though not such glorious use, in my own lesser manner and department. The great virtues, the great vices excite strong enthusiasm, vehement horror, but after all it is not so necessary to warn the generality of mankind against these, either by precept or example, as against lesser faults.[2]

Having come to her literary maturity at a time when the ubiquitous and unvarying stated defence of the novel was its educative power, Maria Edgeworth was among the few authors who truly espoused the educator's role; only her first novel, *Castle Rackrent* (1800), seems to have escaped her desire "to warn the generality of mankind ... against lesser faults." The rest are normally and socially didactic in the extreme.

A close analysis of the alterations which Miss Edgeworth's style underwent when it was pressed into the service of overt didacticism should serve to illuminate the relationship between prose technique and didactic purpose in her work. One's impression upon a first reading of several Edgeworthian novels is that the change from the first to the later is a decline, a drop from *Rackrent's* well-manipulated first person rhetoric and robust Irish vernacular into the smooth, flaccid banalities of the polite popular novel.

The omniscient author's voice in *The Absentee* has a bland accent, his language completely free of colloquial or individualizing idiosyncrasies, his syntax carefully and moderately balanced, paralleled, made symmetrical. Nothing could distinguish it from the style of any half-dozen polite novels of the period. Thady's voice, on the other hand, is decidedly his own and decidedly suited to his tale. While for Maria Edgeworth the most notable characteristic of Irish speech was its use of figurative language,[3] she succeeds with Thady through the more basic element, syntax.

The whole of *Castle Rackrent* runs rapidly forward through asymmetry and parataxis. There is little subordination and no attempt at balance; Thady's favourite conjunction is "and," as often as not employed illogically, effecting no ideational ligature between two clauses "My son Jason had 'em all handed over to him, and the pressing letters were all unread by Sir Condy" (52). Similarly, syntactically subordinate clauses do not necessarily reflect a real subordination of thought but are often merely another way for Thady to pin a fact to a preceding fact and get on with the story "This nettling him, which it was hard to do, he replied" (51). The heavy employment of absolute constructions tends to the same end: it gives the impression of a mind which makes few distinctions. Thady talks along amiably and rapidly, while the temporal sequence of his narrative acts as the only structuring principle in his thought. How clearly his language habits reveal his thinking habits is evident in the continuation of the passage quoted above: "The pressing letters were all unread by Sir Condy, who hated trouble, and could never be brought to hear talk of business" (52). the neat definition of business as trouble unconsciously effected by the syntax of the apposition is an indication of how, in the course of the novel, one comes to understand Thady's identification with the Rackrent family, whose prejudices he not only defends, but shares. A description of Thady's speech is a picture of the novel's world, its refusal to see causality, to make choices, to think. Miss Edgeworth's decision to abandon that world for more conventional realms was a decided loss to literature.

In Thady's milieu, all the language has, besides a brogue, the servant accent. Miss Edgeworth doubtless justified this, rightly, on the grounds that all was being reported by Thady and would therefore have this tone. Had the novel been cast in the third person, we might well have been subjected to a Sir Condy speaking in parallel clauses.[4]

There is, in *Castle Rackrent*, some representation of social stratification through speech, on quite realistic grounds, in contradistinction to the mechanical separations of the polite novel. The representative of the lowest caste who has much to say in the novel is Judy M'Quirk:

Judy made a sign to me, and I went over to the door to her, and she said — 'I wonder to see Sir Condy so low! — Has he heard the news?' 'What news?' says I. — 'Didn't ye hear it, then? (says she) my lady Rackrent that what is kilt* and lying for dead, and I don't doubt but it's all over with her by this time.' — 'Mercy on us all, (says I) how was it?' — 'The jaunting car it was that that ran away with her, (says Judy). — I was coming home that same time from Biddy M'Guggin's marriage, and a great crowd of people too upon the road coming from the fair of Crookaghnawatur, and I sees a jaunting car standing in the middle of the road, and with the two wheels off and all tattered. — What's this? says I.' — 'Didn't ye hear of it? (says they that were looking on) it's my lady Rackrent's car that was running away from her husband, and the horse took fright at a carrion that lay across the road, and so ran away with the jaunting car, and my lady Rackrent and her maid screaming, and the horse ran with them against a car that was coming from the fair, with the boy asleep on it, and the lady's petticoat hanging out of the jaunting car caught, and she was dragged I can't tell you how far upon the road, and it all broken up with the stones just going to be pounded, and one of the road makers with his sledge hammer in his hand stops the horse at the last; but my lady Rackrent was all kilt and smashed, and they lifted her into a cabin hard by, and the maid was found after, where she had been thrown, in the gripe of the ditch, her cap and bonnet all full of bog water — and they say my lady can't live any way. Thady, pray now is it true what I'm told for sartain, that Sir Condy has made over all to your son Jason (84-86)?

What separates Judy's speech from Sir Condy's and Sir Kit's is largely dialect characteristics. Miss Edgeworth was well acquainted with the Irish peasant through her father's tenantry, and there is none of Mrs Radcliffe's literary low speech in her representation of their language. Like Betty, Judy makes elisions and favours the present tense, depicting her action as quick and dramatic. Her speech also accurately exemplifies the Irish idiom, particularly in the omission of the finite verb "and a great crowd of people too upon the road," "and with two wheels off and all tattered," "and it all broken up with the stones" (85). This trick of syntax, the one element of Irish speech sure to be found in any half-decent attempt at the dialect, always occurs in what, if the verb were stated, would be a coordinate clause, frequently the third or fourth in a chain of loose paratactic members. It seems most frequently to be an omission of a form of the verb "to be" and succeeds in laying a heavy stress on the subject, thus emphasizing the concrete and immediate quality of a language which relies heavily on active verbals, progressive presents, and nouns. It is something of this quality that Miss Edgeworth stresses in her emphasis on active verbs and concrete metaphors in her analysis of the Dublin shoeblack's speech (*Essay on Irish Bulls,* 190-195).

Judy's speech reflects more of her own mind than does that of Peter or of Betty, and in doing so gives us a portrait in miniature of the whimsical vision of the novel, for she mirrors on her level the moral world of the whole Rackrent tribe, lords and servants, from old Sir Patrick O'Shaughlin down to Jason Quirk. Her mind is not only concrete and active, it is also totally incapable of making distinctions. Her paratactical selection of details underscores her complete amorality: she runs through the details of the jaunting-car incident, giving them all equal value, so that my Lady Rackrent's smashed limbs stand on the same footing as the maid's "cap and bonnet all full of bog water." The juxtaposition of the last question put to Thady to "my lady can't live anyway" (besides calling into question the value of formulaic possessive pronouns) caps and crystallizes the moral obliquity of the *Rackrent* world. Actions and motivation throughout the novel display the same quality, Thady's own financial justification of all things sacred and profane being outdone only by his son's. Yet all the events, from the imprisonment of Sir Kit's Jewish wife to the death of Sir Condy, horrible as they may be in fact, are as funny in the telling as Judy's rehearsal of Bella's accident — because of the irony of the telling.

The author's pedagogic instinct never again allowed her to run the risk of reader misunderstanding that an unreliable narrator (Judy, Thady) and good irony must always involve. Even with the help of explicating footnotes, the reader of the later novels is not trusted to draw conclusions. The Irish peasants of *The Absentee,* while they stand far above their anglicized masters in point of realism and interest, have lost the individuality of the *Rackrent* world as well as its amorality and have instead a large portion of pure sentiment. Their dialect is as accurately transcribed, but it is a transcription and not art; it says nothing to the reader but that he now is in Ireland among the good-hearted peasants. A welcome change from the priggishness of Lord Colambre's eternally correct periods, the peasant dialect is the most realistic speech of *The Absentee,* but that is all it is, its strongest effect being its power to throw the falsity of Colambre's idiom into high relief.

The convention which Maria Edgeworth has adopted and worked to death in *The Absentee* and her other didactic works is, as I have pointed out, basic to the eighteenth-century novel,[5] but its roots lie in the drama, tracing at least to the Renaissance separation of high and low characters by their forms of speech.[6] Throughout the eighteenth-century drama, and most noticeably in the sentimental comedy, the separation becomes more and more a means of moral judgment as well as social identification. In Ben Jonson, Lady Dashfort would have as much right to speak with flawless grammar as Lord Colambre, but in Cumberland's *West Indian,* Lady Rusport does speak on Lady Dashfort's level, and Belcour, with the disadvantage of a minority spent in the West Indies, speaks like Colambre. Men of sense as early as Steele's Bevel in *The Conscious Lovers* share the Colambre idiom; accepting it as true speech must have represented an immensely willing suspension of disbelief. That Miss Edgeworth herself was willing to accept Johnsonian periods in the midst of idiomatic English even in a novelistic setting is apparent from her comment on Mrs Inchbald's *Simple Story,* which exploits the convention much as *The Absentee* does:

> I was so carried away by it that I was totally incapable of thinking of Mrs Inchbald or anything but Miss Milner and Doriforth, who appeared to me real persons whom I saw and heard, and who had such power to interest me, that I cried my eyes almost out (*Letters,* p. 213).

This ability to accept Miss Milner's crisis allows romance, stage histrionics, and a mechanical plot to pass by without upsetting the effect concentrated in the moral lesson that these things are rigged to service. It represents a staggering quantity of poetic faith surprising in a woman so deaf to poetry, so literal-minded in language, and so devoted to the positive realism she found in the Irish peasantry.

The only coherent reason for Miss Edgeworth's acceptance is, I think, the appeal of didactic moralism. In the first place, she is willing to suspend judgment — and expects the same of her reader — wherever the service of the moral is the result. Everything else may go so long as the lesson is enforced. The lesson might be a warning against moral impropriety, as in Miss Milner's story, or against social injustice, as in *The Absentee*. Furthermore, the whole reliance on positive exemplars, however unrealistic, had been justified long before by Steele, who argued that the stage must supply perfect heroes since its examples are imitated and since simple natures are incapable of making the necessary deductions from the negative exemplars of satire.[7]

The exemplary method, first lauded by Jeremy Collier, then popularized by Steele, was, as John Harrington Smith points out, rampant in all types of literature through the time of Sterne.[8] It seems to me that Miss Edgeworth, decades later, is as fully commited to the method as Collier could have wished anyone to be.

Maria Edgeworth could leave her peasants relatively real (while carefully dissociating herself from them) since they are not required to carry much of the didactic burden. Sentimentalized and condescended to, they escape the exemplary role assigned to the hero and heroine and thereby escape their betters' priggishness of manner and style. The ultimate speech, the idiom of the people of sense, represents the rule of reason, the ultimate moral doctrine urged in the novel. The fact that Miss Edgeworth's complete approbation is with the hero is underscored by her employing for the voice of the omniscient author Colambre's idiom, identifying her standards implicitly with his. The distribution of the dialogue styles is a rationalist's distribution. What ought reasonably to be said is said. Maria Edgeworth was not the first to reason so: her literary forbears include a distinguished line of Renaissance and Neo-Classical practitioners. Nor did she always reason so: the dynamic, if decadent, voice of Thady Quirk is a debt to art, not rationalism.

THE DIDACTICISM OF EDGEWORTH'S
CASTLE RACKRENT[1]

Gerry H. Brookes

Castle Rackrent is often preferred among Maria Edgeworth's works because it seems a creation free of her usual didacticism, a slice of Irish life presented without comment. "In *Castle Rackrent*," says O. Elizabeth McWhorter Harden, "Miss Edgeworth drew directly from nature; only in *Castle Rackrent* was she a poet."[2] In her major biography, *Maria Edgeworth: A Literary Biography*, Marilyn Butler argues that the story "evolved from a fairly elaborate verbal imitation of a real man" and that the details of the story are arranged, in contrast with her usual practice, around "the character sketch of Thady rather than a didactic theme."[3] Yet there is another view of *Castle Rackrent*, that the book is a powerful condemnation of Irish landlords. Thomas Flanagan, for example, calls the story, "as final and damning a judgment as English fiction has ever passed on the abuse of power and the failure of responsibility."[4]

Flanagan seems closer to the truth here. The story is not a spontaneous imitation of natural events; its subject matter is plainly shaped and carefully evaluated.[5] While the story lacks the explicit moralizing of many of Edgeworth's works, *Castle Rackrent* is implicitly and forcefully didactic, and its success lies in the unique harmony Edgeworth achieved among intention, subject matter, and form.

Castle Rackrent is an act of exemplifying. It is a kind of apologue or moral fable, designed to demonstrate by means of fictional examples that through "quickness, simplicity, cunning, carelessness, dissipation, disinterestedness, shrewdness, and blunder" the Rackrent family has succeeded in destroying its members, its estate, and its dependents, and in disrupting the social order on which its position has depended. *Castle Rackrent* is didactic in form in that it takes its shape from a thesis about or attitudes towards the Irish predicament, not from, say, a plot.[6] Its form is coherent, and the story is plainly a made thing that does not simply reflect the shapelessness of life. For example, the episodic nature of the narrative, which has seemed to some a sign of lack of coherence, is essential to the form. The whole disaster, Edgeworth shows, is brought about by men with certain traits of character operating in a degenerate social order. And an episodic narrative is essential to exemplifying different men with analogous traits causing decline in the family's fortune through time.

The understanding and attitudes that Edgeworth shapes toward these fictional examples are by no means simple. The reader is led to think that the character of the Irish past and the remains of that past in the present render Irish landlords and their tenants particularly unfit to cope with the present, especially in the form of the self-aggrandizing cunning of a Jason Quirk, the middleman.[7] On the other hand, Edgeworth shows that the Irish, self-destructive as they have been, are more colourful, eccentric, and interesting than those who take advantage of them and than the "British manufacturers" who may come after the Union to offer Ireland at least decent management (97). Furthermore, the vestiges of feudal virtues, resident in the social order, which the Rackrents travesty by their conduct, will also be lost entirely. While these virtues, especially loyalty, honour, bravery, a sense of family and place, and generosity, are present largely as values that the Rackrents have no longer or have only in a debased form, the reader may regret their passing. Edgeworth is less sentimental about them than Scott or Burke, more firmly on the side of industry and a pedestrian order, but she does use them to help measure the fall of the Rackrents and to help locate the condition of the Irish she represents.

The reader's understanding of the situation of these characters is qualified by the attitudes created by Edgeworth's examples. The characters are consistently foolish, but the destruction they work on themselves, and on those around them, is more than even they deserve.[8] The effect of *Castle Rackrent* is to provoke a peculiar combination of laughter at and pity for the predicament of these Irish landlords and their tenants and, at the same time, to make the reader see the causes of that predicament in the mental and moral confusion of the Irish, which is in turn caused by their own traits of character and encouraged by the degenerate social system they have inherited.

These ideas and attitudes are exemplified by an episodic history of the decline of the Rackrent family, beginning with the assumption of the name by Sir Patrick and ending with its demise at the death of Sir Condy. Each generation has its particular vices.

Sir Patrick is a genial entertainer and powerful drinker. He dies in a fit after a drinking bout, belying the song he sang earlier in the evening about the relative virtue of going to bed drunk. He is imprudent in his liquor and in his management of the estate, and at the last his corpse is seized for his debts.

His successor, Sir Murtagh, is a hard, penurious man, who refuses to ransom his father's body, on the dubious ground that he would pay debts of honour, but since the law was involved, it was no longer a question of honour. Sir Murtagh further distinguishes himself by making the first of the family's succession of bad marriages. He weds a puritanical Miss Skinflint, who turns out to be more penny-pinching than he. Though they disagree about Sir Murtagh's proclivity for good food, they co-operate to make life miserable for the tenantry, taking advantage of them in every available way. He hastens his own ruin, however, through numerous foolish law suits, and dies of a broken blood vessel, provoked by an argument with his wife about an abatement. She and the money for which he married her survive him, and the healthy jointure she takes with her debilitates the estate further.

Sir Kit, Sir Murtagh's younger brother, and heir to Castle Rackrent, displays different vices. He is a young rake and milks the tenants through an agent to support his prodigal ways. He, too, marries badly for money, and his abused Jewish wife survives him. His way with women leads directly to his death at the hands of a representative of the third woman who claimed he had made false promises to her.

Sir Condy, the last Rackrent, is a throwback to Sir Patrick, whom he honours with a new tombstone. He chooses to marry for money, rather than for love, by flipping a coin. This wife is wasteful and extravagant, and she brings him to the brink of ruin. Showing some cunning, he saves himself briefly by getting elected to Parliament, free of his debtors' claims. The progressive financial ruin of the estate falls full upon him, and he dies abandoned by all.

Each character has his own weaknesses, and they all share the inability to manage their lives and their property. Regardless of their attitude toward the estate and its tenants, generous in Sir Patrick's and Sir Condy's cases, careless in Sir Kit's, and predatory in Sir Murtagh's, each manages Castle Rackrent badly, creating a legacy of waste and debt. Their attempts to compensate for their stupidity and incompetence by marrying wealth are in each case frustrated and self-destructive. Especially in marriage the family makes itself susceptible to fortune or "luck," represented most graphically in Sir Condy's act of flipping a coin to decide whom he will marry.

The family also makes itself susceptible to Jason Quirk, who rises with a vengeance from the side of his father, the faithful family retainer, to near control of the estate. Jason is not a paragon of business virtues set against the wastefulness of his former masters, but he has a kind of managerial cunning which they lack and to which they render themselves victims. He is selfish and self-aggrandizing, a wholly unattractive figure. He is, however, important in Edgeworth's scheme to show both how the Rackrent family destroys itself and what agencies will hasten that destruction. She uses Jason as an agent of the family's ruin and also to control the reader's attitudes toward the Rackrent family. As suggested above, the family represents vestiges of a social order that is degenerate and obsolete. This older order, however, even in its degenerate state, is colourful, eccentric, occasionally generous and honourable. Its perpetuation, on the other hand, is dangerous, because it causes suffering among the tenantry, because it is wasteful and self-destructive, and because it creates and encourages aggressive, selfish men like Jason. The passing of the old order with its scant virtues and astonishing eccentricity would be less mourned if one had any assurance that a better order than Jason's would succeed it. Edgeworth holds out some hope in the end: "It is a problem of difficult solution to determine, whether an Union will hasten or retard the amelioration of this country. The few gentlemen of education who now reside in this country will resort to England: they are few, but they are in nothing inferior to men of the same rank in Great Britain. The best that can happen will be the introduction of British manufacturers in their places" (97). But it seems a meagre hope.

The effect of *Castle Rackrent* is intellectual and ethical. The story presents examples which provoke understanding and judgment. The effect is also emotional. Edgeworth constructs her narrative in such a way that the reader is made to laugh at and also to pity the Irish characters from a felt position of superiority. This response is shaped by the facts of the narrative, the action and speech of the characters and the rewards and punishments accorded them. It is also evoked by the artful manipulation of the voice of Thady

Quirk, the loyal servant who narrates the tale.

Thady has always been recognized as Edgeworth's finest achievement, and he is crucial to the effects of her apologue. First of all, he is used as an example of the ways in which the wastefulness of the Rackrent family affects those who depend on them.[9] As he tells us, he has descended from "Honest Thady" through "Old Thady" to "Poor Thady" as a result of the family's decline. He is also useful to Edgeworth in bringing to bear loyalty and a sense of family as ideals that the Rackrents fail to abide by.[10]

More importantly, Thady represents an affecting kind of mental and moral confusion that is at the heart of the predicament of the Irish characters in this story. The confusion manifests itself in several ways, in the ironic, implicit judgments that Edgeworth makes of characters through Thady, in the kinds of errors in judgment and sense that Thady makes that reflect solely on him, and in his uncomprehending narration of the stupidity of others. In *Essay on Irish Bulls,* prepared with her father's help, Edgeworth defines a bull as *"a laughable confusion of ideas."*[11] This description captures the state of the Irish mind in *Castle Rackrent,* except that our response to it is not simply laughter, but laughter mixed with pity. Thady himself commits a number of bulls.[12] His remark that the Rackrents' old family name was "O'Shaughlin, related to the kings of Ireland — but that was before my time" is an example. Here Thady's naïve confusion about the past is innocent and laughable enough, but his kind of confusion is continuous with more serious sorts that are both laughable and pitiable.

Sir Tallyhoo Rackrent's situation, for example, is more serious. He "had a fine estate of his own, only never a gate upon it, it being his maxim, that a car was the best gate. — Poor gentleman! he lost a fine hunter and his life, at last, by it, all in one day's hunt" (9). The confusion manifests itself here in a form like wit. The shift in sense of the verb "lost" between its first object, "hunter," and the second, "life," and, more importantly, the violation of the reader's expectations by the second object, is a kind of zeugma. The casual tidiness with which his carelessness is avenged is likewise surprising, unsettling, and amusing, though one glimpses uneasily through the laughter a world in which hunters and lives are lost with nearly equal regret, "all in one day's hunt." The world the characters inhabit is like this, a vengeful world. The consequences of carelessness, of improvidence, are severe. And these consequences, the reader sees, attend mental and moral confusion of the sort that Edgeworth represents in Thady's speech and in what he reports. Being led to judgment, through laughter and pity, makes the reader aware of an intelligence arranging the fictions before him, makes him aware of what Wayne Booth has called the "implied author," that is, the author implicit in the style and form of the story.[13] And Thady is one of the main devices by which judgments of characters and events are caused. The wit involved in Thady's witless narration makes the reader feel superior to its perpetrator, makes him share with the author the sense of superiority of a mind ordered sufficiently to see the mistake that is being made. The reader is made to think that, in such circumstances, he would know better.

In *Irish Bulls* the Edgeworths show that bulls are closely related to rhetorical figures and that the susceptibility of the Irish to bulls is related directly to their habitual use of colourful language. In *Castle Rackrent* the characters are victimized by their figurative language to some extent, and at the same time they are made more interesting and attractive by it. The bulls in *Castle Rackrent* place the reader in the position of the critic of rhetoric who knows the figures and where they have gone awry. When Thady remarks that Jason sticks to Sir Condy, as Thady "could not have done at the time, if you'd have given both the Indies and Cork to boot," he creates an example of bathos (74). Yet the humour of his remark is assimiliated, as is true throughout, to the particular thesis of *Castle Rackrent*. Thady's bathetic bull is rooted in his parochialism, which is one cause of the Irish predicament.

In a footnote Edgeworth informs us of another "mode of rhetoric common in Ireland" (105). Thady has remarked of Sir Murtagh, "Out of forty-nine suits which he had, he never lost one but seventeen" (15). Edgeworth notes that in such cases, "an astonishing assertion is made in the beginning of a sentence, which ceases to be in the least surprizing, when you hear the qualifying explanation that follows" (105). The remarkable achievement of Sir Murtagh turns out, as usual, not to be remarkable at all. Some of the humour of *Castle Rackrent* depends on figurative language, of the sort that concerns the Edgeworths in *Irish Bulls,* but much of it is syntactical humour, of the sort just quoted.[14] Words and phrases are arranged in order to create expectations of one sort that are then undercut by implications of a different sort. Some examples of this kind of wit are periodic sentences. Thady says of Sir Condy, "Born to little or no fortune of his own, he was bred to the bar, at which having many friends to push him, and no mean natural abilities of his own, he doubtless would in process of time, if he could have borne the drudgery of that study, have been rapidly made king's counsel at the least — But things were disposed of otherwise, and he never went the circuit but twice, and then made no figure for want of a fee, and being unable to speak in public" (38). The accumulating qualifications here are devastating. Pretentious expectations for Sir Condy are set up and then destroyed by the pathetic and laughable actualities of his abilities and situation.

The wit of figures and syntax is consistently heightened by the large context of the reader's increasingly more comprehensive vision of the mental and moral confusion of the Irish. Edgeworth presents to the reader a series of examples of men making both errors in judgment, which reveal themselves as verbal foolishness, and errors in action, based on mistaken judgment. In *Irish Bulls* Edgeworth's phrase for the latter is "practical bulls" (p. 12). The practical bulls committed by the Rackrents are the most likely acts of confusion to create pity as well as laughter in the reader, because they have effects on persons and because they bring severe punishment on their perpetrators. Sir Kit's fate is probably the worst, and Edgeworth catches his misery in a phrase. In good spirits, he lets an opponent off in a duel, knocking a tooth-pick out of his fingers. But, "unluckily," he is hit himself "in a vital part, and was brought home, in little better than an hour after the affair, speechless, on a hand-barrow, to my lady" (33). He has done what his family constantly does, exposed himself to luck. Sir Condy gambles in choosing a wife and later gambles on his wife's death. Sir Murtagh goes to law, and, as a footnote tells us, that is a kind of lottery (109). Relying on luck in the providential world of an Edgeworth tale is tempting the rational god of industry in the worst possible way. Salvation in her stories comes through all of the qualities missing in the Irish of *Castle Rackrent*, through honesty, patience, industry, practical knowledge, humility.[15] No one is rewarded much in *Castle Rackrent* because no one has the requisite virtues, but we are meant to feel their absence. We are meant to think Ireland needed those "few gentlemen of education who now reside in this country," needed, Edgeworth must have thought, practical people like herself and her father.

Castle Rackrent is, then, an act of exemplifying, and its parts are shaped to demonstrate the truth of Edgeworth's view of the situation of the Irish and to create an ethical and emotional atttitude toward them and their predicament. The story does not simply represent but evaluates through a variety of rhetorical means.

This description of the form of the work has several uses. First of all, describing the story as an apologue, as something different from most of the works we call novels, can preserve us from seeing certain qualities of the book, such as inconsistencies in the representation of Thady and the episodic nature of the narrative, as weaknesses in it.[16] It can also prevent us from looking for qualities of plot normally found in novels. In *Maria Edgeworth the Novelist, 1767-1849: A Bicentennial Study,* James Newcomer, in order to explain Thady's incredible combination of naiveté at times and his remarkable shrewdness at others, argues that, in fact, Thady is shrewd and deceitful throughout, that he plots in collusion with his son to overthrow the Rackrent family.[17] This view plainly misuses evidence, but it is the sort of explanation encouraged by a misperception of the form of the tale and by a misunderstanding of the principles operating within it.[18] If one looks for qualities ordinarily found in novels, consistent development of character, suspense about the fates of characters, then one will be led to extravagant theses like Newcomer's, or one will conclude that this is a badly managed novel.

This description of *Castle Rackrent* as an apologue clarifies both why the work is not objective and historical and why it is taken to be so. The story may represent a view of a particular historical situation that is accurate and can be tested empirically, but our appreciation of its having done so is external to our apprehension of the form of the story. Edgeworth presents fictional examples and not history. Her intention is to shape our attitudes and beliefs toward what we perceive as fictional men in fictional situations and to urge us to make the same judgment of actual men in actual situations. This distinction is crucial for understanding the form of the book and the working of that form. As mentioned above, most of those who argue that the book is a direct portrait of Irish life acknowledge that the picture that comes full blown through the neutral medium of the artist is, somehow, not a flattering one.

Ernest A. Baker, for example, in *The History of the Novel*, says that Edgeworth "gave imagination full fling, and did not let any idea of a purpose interfere, although the favourite moral theme is implicit, the nemesis of self-indulgence, extravagance, and folly, as it must needs be in such a register of tragedy" (p. 28). But the work is purposeful, and our understanding and pleasure are dependent on our perception of that didactic, exemplificative purpose. We are stirred by what we perceive as examples of mental and moral confusion. The "moral theme" is not simply "implicit"; it is the cause of our pleasure in reading.

Castle Rackrent is not history, not a psychological case study, not a work which by its form demands empirical verification. If we say, even hypothetically, that it is an apologue, then we can deduce that the characters, including the narrator, will serve the attitudes being shaped. They will seem life-like or take on the kinds of expectations we have for characters in most novels only up to the point at which those features interfere with exemplification of the central attitudes.[19] We can deduce, for example, that what Thady says will be determined by a desire to represent character but that representation of his character will be subordinated to a need to exemplify certain ideas and to shape attitudes. In reading history or a psychological case history, we would perceive this shaping as a flaw. In the case of *Castle Rackrent* the perception that the author is creating and shaping fictional examples is inescapable, and it allows the form to work.

Writing history would make demands on Edgeworth that she does not have to fulfil. She has greater ease in inventing and arranging examples than a historian has. She can create a narrator with some qualities of regional speech and ignorance, but she can manipulate his voice to serve her purpose. In fact, the manipulation of his voice is one of the clues, necessary to her form, that we are reading fiction and not history. The attitudes embedded by the story may be treated subsequently against the actual, and if they hold up, then we will say that she has provided us with a proper historical view.[20] The power of this form is that it can provide us with complex attitudes that we seem to have induced from particular examples, so that when we turn to the actual, we know what sorts of evidence will confirm our now deductive model.

Edgeworth's ability to make us induce from fictional examples ideas that seem plausible when tested against the actual is one cause of the view that she has written history. Another cause is her ability to create life-likeness within the confines of her form. She cannot allow Thady to become as absorbing or as boring as an actual Irishman might be, but she can and does make him vivid and engaging, while he serves the exemplificative and evaluative functions essential to the form. There are two other apparent reasons for thinking she might be representing the actual. The first is the constant reference of her notes and glossary to the actual. They insist that the fictions are not implausible since real events like them have occurred. They tend to generalize her examples, and they encourage testing the hypothetical view of the Irish situation created by the story against historical occurrences. The second reason is Edgeworth's own insistence that the story came to her spontaneously, that she heard the voice of an old steward speaking to her and simply recorded it.[21] This external evidence is usually linked with two other observations to create an explanation of the genesis of the story that makes it seem simply a slice of life. *Castle Rackrent* was written without the aid or interference, depending on your point of view, of her father, and it lacks the explicit moralizing of her other works, virtually all of which she wrote under his guidance. Free of her father's restraining hand, this romantic argument goes, she could see life clearly and record it without comment.[22] To the contrary she seems to have been free to create a more successful didactic form which embedded judgments and attitudes in examples and did not grind to a halt, as many of her other stories do, to make explicit what is (or ought to be) implicit in her fictions.

Behind the traditional uneasiness about the relation of *Castle Rackrent* to Edgeworth's other works may also be a notion that it is not didactic because it does not display virtue. The story shows, as Dr. Johnson thought narratives should, "that vice is the natural consquence of narrow thoughts, that it begins in mistake, and ends in ignominy," but it does not, as the Doctor would have it, exemplify virtue, except by its absence. To some extent the demands of what Dr. Johnson calls "historical veracity" militated against the display of virtue.[23] Still, the lack of neoclassical moral balance may be a source of continued uneasiness about the work.[24] In 1803 Richard Lovell Edgeworth remarked somewhat defensively, "What we have already published has always tended to improve the education of our country: even *Castle Rackrent* has that object remotely in mind."[25] The emphasis on vice and not on virtue in the tale is enough to explain his hesitation about the story. He does recognize its didactic nature, and there seems to be no evidence to support Marilyn Butler's claim that *Castle Rackrent* is fundamentally different from Maria Edgeworth's other books, that the story is not coherent because Thady's character takes precedence over the author's progressive point of view, and that the Edgeworths rejected the tale, at least for a time, because it did not say what Maria Edgeworth wished (see Butler, esp. pp. 306-307, 359-360). Instead the Edgeworths seem to have recognized its nature and power quite clearly and to have been visibly relieved, as they say in *Irish Bulls,* that the "generosity" of the Irish had let *Castle Rackrent* among them be "generally taken merely as good-humoured raillery, not as insulting satire" (p. 184). The risk that the Irish might take the book more seriously is, of course, implicit in the intention it embodies.

Castle Rackrent stands out from Edgeworth's other stories, not, as some have claimed, by being non-didactic, but by the particular harmony in it of intention, subject matter, and form. The importance of her subject matter should not be overlooked. As Joanne Altieri has shown, Edgeworth's subjects here permit her greater verbal play and more complex stylistic effects than do the more rational subjects of her other stories. Of course, our pleasure in the vernacular is complicated further by the evaluations of it and its speakers that are implicit in every level of the form, especially in syntax and situation.

Many of her stories go awry because they fail to embody a coherent intention and are perceived as mixed or flawed forms. Her apologues are marred by their tendency to break out into plotted novels, into imitations of actions, and her plotted novels are marred by her persistent desire to reduce the complexity of human interactions to aphoristic examples. *The Absentee,* to take an obvious case, is flawed formally because Edgeworth's desire to exemplify the need for absentee Irish landlords to return to their land interferes with her efforts to create hopes and fears for the fate of that paragon, Lord Colambre. There is little doubt that he will succeed in everything he desires, and the plot focuses instead on how he will achieve it. The signals, however, are so clear that happiness resides on the land in Ireland, that one knows all he has to do is to lure his family home. Then, of course, some fortuitous circumstance will reveal Grace Nugent's legitimacy, and all will be well. Edgeworth's faith in the power of virtuous conduct to regulate human affairs and to create happiness is so strong that she has difficulty in making her reader feel satisfaction in seeing a foregone conclusion work itself out. Her beliefs work against subtle plots and encourage a tendency to exemplify. When, for example, Colambre asks a friend whether he should join the army, he cannot ask about his own situation: "Would you advise me — I won't speak of myself, because we judge better by general views than by particular cases — would you advise a young man at present to go into the army?" (*Tales and Novels*, 6:222). Her consistent interest is in general views.

Vice, however, seems not to be bound by such rigid rules, and it constantly enlivens her stories, even the moral fables intended to instruct the young.[26] There her evil characters, since they are motivated by probability rather than moral necessity, create suspense that distracts, happily, from the ideas she is trying to exemplify. Hazlitt remarked that except for *Castle Rackrent* her stories "are a kind of pedantic, pragmatical common sense, tinctured with the pertness and pretensions of the paradoxes to which they are so self-complacently opposed."[27] In *Castle Rackrent* she manages harmony between her evaluation of the Irish situation and the fictions she creates to exemplify it. Her examples correspond to the complexity of her view and give us complex pleasure.[28]

NOTES

Preface

1. (London: Oxford U P, 1964, 1969, 1980). This edition is cited throughout this collection.
2. See Watson's note, xxvii-xxviii.
3. Marilyn Butler, *Maria Edgeworth: A Literary Biography* (London: Oxford U P, 1972). Cited as Butler below.
4. "Memoirs of the family of Edgeworth since the Revolution in 1688," 3 vols.; and "Memoirs ... of the Edgeworth family," 1 vol., National Library of Ireland, MSS 7361-7364. H. J. and H. E. Butler, eds., *The Black Book of Edgeworthstown and Other Edgeworth Memories, 1585-1817* (London: Faber: 1927).
5. Butler 16.
6. Butler 174.
7. National Library of Ireland, MS 7361: 193-94. This is omitted from the published *Black Book of Edgeworthstown*. Cf. 17-37.
8. MS 7362, 179-80.
9. Richard Lovell Edgeworth and Maria Edgeworth, *An Essay on Irish Bulls* (London: J. Johnson, 1802, 1803) 305-06.
10. Emily Lawless, *Maria Edgeworth* (London: Macmillan, 1904). For Gwynn, see Bibliography.

Maria Edgeworth 1768-1849 by John Cronin

1. Reprinted from *The Anglo-Irish Novel. Vol 1: The Nineteenth Century* (Belfast: Appletree, 1980) 21-24, with the author's permission and the kind consent of the publishers.
2. "Maria Edgeworth's Irish Novels," *Studies 27* (1938): 558. An excerpt is reprinted below [Ed.].

The Sources and Composition of *Castle Rackrent* by

Marilyn Butler

1. Reprinted with permission of author and publisher, Oxford University Press, from *Maria Edgeworth: A Literary Biography* (London: Oxford U P, 1972) 240-43, 352-60.
2. Maria Edgeworth to Mrs Stark, 6 Sept. 1834, Harriet Butler and Lucy Robinson, *Memoir of Maria Edgeworth* 3 vols. (privately printed, 1867) 3:152. Maria Edgeworth borrowed twice from the Langan family: John's granddaughter Kitty was the original of Simple Susan. Maria Edgeworth to Charles Sneyd Edgeworth, 4 april 1808, and *Memoir* 1:284.
3. Maria Edgeworth to Sophy Ruxton, 22 Jan. 1794.
4. The full story is told in *The Gentleman's Magazine*, lix (1789):766-67, and by Edward Ford, *Tewin-Water: or the story of Lady Cathcart* (Enfield, 1876).
5. Maria Edgeworth to Mrs Stark, 6 Sept. 1834, *Memoir* 3:152-53. County Fermanagh is not, however, in the neighbourhood of Edgeworthstown.
6. See Butler 16n.
7. Richard Lovell Edgeworth to David Augustus Beaufort, 26 April 1800.
8. Richard Lovell Edgeworth to Mr Frederick, 25 June 1812, and note in Maria

Edgeworth's hand on back fly-leaf of a Butler copy of the 1st ed. of *Castle Rackrent* (see George Watson's edition, Appendix A). Similar incidents occur elsewhere in eighteenth-century memoirs, and also in folk stories, but the Edgeworth version seems reasonably reliable, in that it emanates from Richard Edgeworth [Maria Edgeworth's grandfather, Ed.]. Another family lawsuit provided the climax of *Patronage*, 4 vols. (London, 1814). See *Patronage*, ch. 12, 398-404 and *Memoirs of Richard Lovell Edgeworth, Esq.; Begun by Himself and Concluded by His Daughter, Maria Edgeworth*, 2 vols. (London, 1820) 1:17-18.

9. Preface, *Castle Rackrent* 4.
10. *Castle Rackrent* 26.
11. *Castle Rackrent* 36.
12. See Butler 120 and *Castle Rackrent* 51 ff. The painter Joseph Farington records that Captain Francis Beaufort told him that *Castle Rackrent* was written "8 years before it was published," entry for March 1819, *Farington Diary*, ed. James Greig (London: Hutchinson, 1928) 8:217. Although Beaufort is in general an unexceptional source, it has to be admitted that Maria Edgeworth was out of Ireland in 1792, and that she did not see Mrs Ruxton, which makes the story difficult to accept as it stands.
13. See Butler 15-16.
14. See introductory note to Glossary 98.
15. Mrs Frances Anne Edgeworth to David Augustus Beaufort, Hill Top, nr. Birmingham, 23 April 1799, National Library of Ireland, MS 13176(4).
16. George Watson, Introduction to *Castle Rackrent* xx.
17. Preface, *Castle Rackrent* 4.
18. Thomas Flanagan, *The Irish Novelists, 1800-1850* (New York: Columbia UP, 1959) 23.
19. Preface, *Castle Rackrent* 4-5.
20. *Castle Rackrent* 20-21.
21. Donald Davie, *The Heyday of Sir Walter Scott* (London: Routledge, 1961) 66.
22. The report of the Leicester bookseller who ran a circulating library. See Butler 188.
23. Richard Lovell Edgeworth to David Augustus Beaufort, 26 April 1800.
24. Richard Lovell Edgeworth to Maria Edgeworth, London, 17 May 1805. Lord Carhampton had been the Irish Commander-in-Chief in 1796-97. See Butler 121.
25. Richard Lovell Edgeworth to David Augustus Beaufort, 26 April 1800.
26. William Beaufort to Mrs Frances Anne Edgeworth, 2 Oct. 1800, National Library of Ireland, MS 13176(5).

Maria Edgeworth and the English Novel by Ernest Baker

1. Vol. VI, *Edgeworth, Austen, Scott* (London: Witherby, 1935) 11-19. Reprinted with the consent of Barnes & Noble Books, Totowa, N. J..
2. "Walter Scott has no business to write novels, especially good ones — It is not fair — He has Fame and Profit enough as a Poet, and should not be taking the bread out of other people's mouths — I do not like him, and do not mean to like *Waverley* if I can help it — but fear I must." *Jane Austen's Letters to her sister Cassandra and others*, ed. R. W. Chapman (Oxford: Oxford U P, 1932), 28 Sept. 1814 404.
3. William Hazlitt, *The Spirit of the Age* (Oxford: Oxford U P, 1904) "Sir Walter Scott."
4. M. Dumont is often mentioned with respect in her letters, and in her last novel, *Helen*, Lady Davenant speaks of him more than once as a man and a writer whose criticism and counsel were fearless and far-sighted. Maria Edgeworth always accepted his criticisms of her own work with deference, and probably benefited by them.
5. Professor J. Macmurray dates this conception from the Cartesian affirmation of self-

consciousness as the reality from which all belief and all theory have their starting-point. *Cogito ergo sum* was at once the foundation-stone of rationalism and the declaration of rights of the individual. "The Unity of Modern Problems," *Journal of Philosophical Studies*, 4 (1929) 14.

6. Charlotte Brontë, *Shirley* (1849).

7. "To him [Burke] a nation was a living organism, of infinitely complex structure, of intimate dependence upon the parts, and to be treated by politicians in obedience to a careful observation of the laws of its healthy development. To them [the French revolutionists] a nation was an aggregate of independent units, to be regulated by a set of absolute *a priori* maxims." Leslie Stephen, *English Thought in the Eighteenth Century*, 2 vols. (London, 1876) 2:248-49.

8. Precedents for her stories for children were furnished by Madame d'Épinay, with her *Les Conversationes d'Émilie* (Leipzig, 1774); Arnaud Berquin, author of *'L'Ami des Enfantes*, 24 vols. (London, 1782-83), and *Le petit Grandison* (Paris, 1787); and also Madame de Genlis, with her *Théâtre d'Éducation*, 4 vols. (Dublin, 1784).

An Early "Irish" Novelist by W. B. Coley

1. Reprinted from *Minor British Novelists*, Charles Alva Hoyt, ed., Harry T. Moore, preface (Carbondale & Edwardsville: Southern Illinois U P, 1967) 17-24, with the permission of the author and Southern Illinois University Press.

The Nature of the Irish Novel by Thomas Flanagan

1. From *The Irish Novelists: 1800-1850* (New York: Columbia U P, 1959), chapter 3, 35-46. Reprinted with the permission of the author and Columbia University Press.

2. John Gibson Lockhart, *Life of Sir Walter Scott, Bart*, 2nd ed. 12 vols. (Edinburgh, 1839) 8:25.

3. "Remorse for Intemperate Speech," *Collected Poems of William Butler Yeats* (New York: Macmillan, 1976) 249.

4. *Castle Rackrent* 96-97.

5. David J. O'Donoghue, preface, First Series of William Carleton, *Traits and Stories of the Irish Peasantry*, 4 vols. (Dublin, 1886) 1:xxiv-xxvi.

6. Lady Morgan, *O'Donnel: A National Tale*, 3 vols. (London, 1814) 1:x.

7. Lady Morgan, *Florence Macarthy: An Irish Tale*, 4 vols. (London, 1863) 1:vi.

8. See, for example, William O'Brien, *Edmund Burke as an Irishman* (Dublin: Gill, 1924).

9. Oliver Goldsmith, "Carolan," *Miscellaneous Writings*, ed. John Prior, 4 vols. (New York, 1850) 4:208-10.

10. It has been put into admirable English verse: *The Midnight Court: A Rhythmical Bacchanalia from the Irish of Bryan Merryman*, tr. Frank O'Connor (Dublin: Fridberg, 1945).

11. "The Memoir of Arthur O'Neill" was first published in full by Charlotte Milligan Fox, *Annals of the Irish Harpers* (London: Smith, Elder, 1911) 137-87. Samuel Ferguson had drawn upon material from the manuscript in preparing the notes to the 1840 edition of Bunting's *Ancient Musick of Ireland*. The passage quoted appears in *Annals* 147.

12. *Annals* 146n.

13. *Annals* 178.

14. *Lady Morgan's Memoirs: Autobiography, Diaries, and Correspondence*, ed. W. Hepworth Dixon, 2nd ed., 2 vols. (London, 1863) 2:293.

15. Hyde, *A Literary History of Ireland* (New York: Scribner's, 1899) ix.

16. Daniel Corkery, *Synge and Anglo-Irish Literature* (Dublin & Cork: Cork U P) 2.
17. Corkery 2.
18. W. J. O'Neill Daunt, *Personal Recollections of Daniel O'Connell,* 2 vols. (London: Chapman, 1848) 1:15.

Castle Rackrent **by Thomas Flanagan**

1. Reprinted with the permission of author and publisher, Columbia University Press from *The Irish Novelists 1800-1850* (New York: Columbia U P, 1959) 69-70, 77-79.
2. Richard Lovell Edgeworth and Maria Edgeworth, *The Memoirs of Richard Lovell Edgeworth, Esq.; Begun by Himself and Completed by His Daughter, Maria Edgeworth,* 2 vols. (London, 1820) 2:5-20.

Maria Edgeworth's *Castle Rackrent* **by Roger McHugh**

1. Reprinted from "Maria Edgeworth's Irish Novels," *Studies* 27 (1938):556-70, with the author's permission and the kind consent of the editor of *Studies.*
2. Introduction to *Selections from Maria Edgeworth* (Dublin: Talbot, n.d.) xx.
3. *Today and Tomorrow in Ireland* (Dublin: Hodges Figgis, 1903) 3-4.
4. Horatio Krans, *Irish Life in Irish Fiction* (New York: Columbia U P, 1903) 28.
5. He voted against the Union, which he desired, because of the methods adopted to pass it.
6. She constantly equated prudence with honour.
7. Gwynn 4.
8. Postscript to *Waverley.* [See General Preface to *Waverley* (1829) ed. Claire Lamont (Oxford: Clarendon, 1981) 352-53, Ed.].
9. *The Letters of Sir Walter Scott* ed. H. J. Grierson, 12 vols. (London: Constable, 1932-37) 5:1142, 15 May 1818.
10. Letter of Maria Edgeworth to Mrs Ruxton, Nov. 21 1811, *Maria Edgeworth: Chosen Letters,* ed. F. V. Barry (Boston & New York: Houghton, 1931) 161.

The Significant Silences of Thady Quirk by Maurice Colgan

1. Reprinted from *Social Roles for the Artist* (Liverpool: Art, Politics, and Society Group, Department of Political Theory and Institutions, University of Liverpool, 1979):41-45, with the author's permission and by kind consent of the publishers.
2. Sir Walter Scott, in chapter 72 of *Waverley* (1814) entitled, "A Postscript which should have been a preface," acknowledges her pioneering role.
3. See *Maria Edgeworth: Chosen Letters,* ed. F. V. Barry (London: n.p., 1931) 243-44.
4. *Castle Rackrent* 33.
5. See Brander Matthews' introduction to his edition of *Castle Rackrent* and *The Absentee* (New York: Dutton, 1952), and Elizabeth Harden, *Maria Edgeworth's Art of Prose Fiction* (The Hague: Mouton, 1971) 60-61. [See selection below, Ed.].
6. Harden 63.
7. *Castle Rackrent* 8-9.
8. *Castle Rackrent* 13.
9. *Castle Rackrent* 28.

10. The Relief Act of 1778 allowed Catholics to take leases of 999 years, but not to purchase land.
11. *Castle Rackrent* 57.
12. Curiously, Maria Edgeworth, in an editorial postscript to the novel, claims that it is being laid before the English reader as "a specimen of life and manners, which are perhaps unknown in England," *Castle Rackrent* 97. The essential facts of Irish life and manners would remain unknown to a reader entirely dependent on *Castle Rackrent* for his information.
13. *Castle Rackrent* 79.
14. *Castle Rackrent* 77.
15. Kenneth Jackson, ed., *A Celtic Miscellany* (Harmondsworth: Penguin, 1971) 222.
16. Butler 112.
17. Butler 96. See also *Memoirs of Richard Lovell Edgeworth, Esq.; Begun by Himself and Concluded by His Daughter, Maria Edgeworth*, 2 vols. (London, 1820), 2, ch. 3.
18. *Castle Rackrent* 97.
19. Published in *Tales of Fashionable Life*, First Series (London: 1809).
20. 19 Feb. 1834, *Chosen Letters* 384.
21. For an account of this episode see Michael Hurst, *Maria Edgeworth and the Public Scene* (London: Macmillan, 1969) 77-86.

"Said an elderly man ...": Maria Edgeworth's Use of Folklore in *Castle Rackrent* by Dáithí Ó hÓgáin

1. Patricia Lysaght, *"An Bhean Chaointe:* The Supernatural Woman in Irish Folklore," *Éire-Ireland* 14, 4 (1979): 7-29.
2. John C. Mac Erlean, *Dunaire Dháibhidh Uí Bhruadair*, 3 vols. (London: Irish Texts Society, 1910-17) 1:36-39.
3. Pádraig Ua Duinnín, *Dánta Phiarais Feiritéir* (Dublin: Foilseacháin Rialtais, 1934) 74, lines 29-32.
4. For a general survey of the otherworld in Irish folklore, see Seán Ó Súilleabháin, *Irish Folk Custom and Belief* (Dublin: Cultural Relations Committee, 1967; Cork: Mercier, 1977) 81-91.
5. See Waldemar Liungman, *Sveriges Sagner*, 7 vols. (Copenhagen: Ejnar Munksgaard, 1957-69) 2, no. 506, 258-69. I owe this reference to Professor Bo Almqvist of the Department of Irish Folklore, University College, Dublin.
6. (London: 1866; Detroit: Singing Tree, 1968) 116-17.
7. I have discussed some such traditions in my article "Gearóid Iarla agus an Draíocht," *Scríobh* 4, ed. Seán Ó Mórdha (Dublin: An Clóchomhar, 1979) 234-59 (especially 243-46). There was, of course, a strong native tradition of trips to the otherworld and to otherworld dwellings. For this, see Myles Dillon, *Early Irish Literature* (Chicago: University of Chicago Press 1948) 101-48; and Seosamh Watson, *Mac na Míchomhairle* (Dublin: An Clóchomhar, 1979) 47-106.
8. Seosamh Laoide, *Sgeálaidhe Oirghiall* (Dublin: Conradh na Gaeilge, 1905) 105-07. Also *Irisleabhar na Gaedhilge*, 11 (October 1901): 168-70.
9. The best study of Irish wakes and death customs is Seán Ó Súilleabháin, *Irish Wakes Amusements* (Cork: Mercier, 1967).
10. Antti Aarne and Stith Thompson, *The Types of the Folktale* (Helsinki: Folklore Fellowship Communications, 1973) 458.
11. The earliest Irish version known to me is from the fourteenth century, and concerns the wizard-poet Mongan, Kuno Meyer, *The Voyage of Bran* (London: Alfred Nutt, 1895)

63-64. Here Mongan stands on two sods of clay and claims thereby to have one foot in Ireland and the other in Scotland. This seems to be related to a version in the life of St Colmcille written by Manas Ó Domhnaill in 1532 — where the saint is described as avoiding the breach of a penitential vow never again to set foot on the soil of Ireland by arriving in Ireland with a Scottish sod under his feet. Ed. A. O'Kelleher and G. Schoepperle *Betha Colaim Chille* (Carbondale: U of Illinois, 1918) 342-45.

12. See Patrick Murray, *Maria Edgeworth* (Cork: Mercier, 1971) 21-22.

Irish Bulls in *Castle Rackrent* by Cóilín Owens

1. *Memoir of Maria Edgeworth*, 3 vols. (privately printed, 1867), 2:241.
2. London: J. Johnson. Citations are to 1803 edition.
3. *A Colder Eye: The Modern Irish Writers* (New York: Knopf, 1983) 3-10.
4. Anonymous. *Teagueland Jests, or Bogg-Witticisms* (London, 1690).
5. *The Irish Comic Tradition* (London: Oxford U P, 1962) 94.
6. *The Ireland of Sir Jonah Barrington from his Personal Sketches*, ed. Hugh Staples (London: Owen, 1968) 248-50.
7. *Personal Sketches* 250.
8. This is a fair assessment of the history of the management of the Edgeworth estate: after his arrival in 1782, Richard Lovell reversed the family traditions of profligacy, neglect and abuse of the tenantry by a programme of reforms which were in advance of any in the country at that time. See Marilyn Butler, *Maria Edgeworth: A Literary Biography* (Oxford: Clarendon, 1972) 1-145.
9. For a survey of these types, see G. C. Duggan, *The Stage Irishman: A History of the Irish Play and Stage Characters from the Earliest Times* (Dublin: Talbot, 1937).
10. Marilyn Butler, *Maria Edgeworth: A Literary Biography* (London: Oxford U P, 1972) 174.

Castle Rackrent: The Disingenuous Thady Quirk by James Newcomer

1. Reprinted from *Maria Edgeworth the Novelist* (Fort Worth: Texas Christian U P, 1967), chapter 9, 144-51, by kind permission of the author and Texas Christian University Press.
2. A. Norman Jeffares in his Introduction to *Maria Edgeworth, Castle Rackrent, Émilie de Coulanges, The Birthday Present* (London and New York: Nelson, 1953) xxiii.
3. Gordon Hall Gerould, *The Patterns of English and American Fiction* (New York: Russell, 1966) 152.
4. Flanagan 69.
5. Flanagan 7.

Transparent Thady Quirk by Elizabeth Harden

1. From Chapter 2, *Maria Edgeworth's Art of Prose Fiction*, by O. Elizabeth McWhorter Harden (The Hague: Mouton, 1971) 55-56, 68-71. Reprinted by kind permission of the author and Mouton Publishers.
2. Horatio Sheafe Krans, *Irish Life in Irish Fiction* (New York: Columbia U P, 1903) 276.
3. Cf. John Galt's *Annals of the Parish* (Edinburgh, 1821). Galt employs the point of view of a single character much in the manner of Maria Edgeworth. An aging minister, Rev.

Micah Balwhidder, is the narrator who chronicles the events of his parish from the time of his appointment until his retirement. Like Thady, he looms large in his own narrative because of his whimsicality and his humorous simplicity, which are augmented by his mellow view of life. Galt's *The Entail* (Edinburgh, 1823) is similar to *Castle Rackrent* in that it covers the fortunes of a family through several generations.

4. *Maria Edgeworth: Chosen Letters*, ed. F. V. Barry (Boston & New York: Houghton, 1931) 243-244.

5. The term "transparency" is used by Brander Matthews to describe Maria Edgeworth's method. See Introduction, *Castle Rackrent* and *The Absentee* (New York: Dutton, 1952) xv.

6. Cited by Percy Howard Newby, *Maria Edgeworth* (Denver: Alan Swallow, 1950) 44.

7. *The Lives of the Novelists* (New York: Dutton, 1910) 376.

8. The phrase is Helen Zimmern's. See *Maria Edgeworth* (Boston, 1884) 74-75.

9. Richard P. Blackmur, Introduction, *The Art of the Novel*, by Henry James (New York: Scribner's, 1962) xi.

10. *The Life and Letters of Maria Edgeworth*, ed. Augustus J. C. Hare, 2 vols. (London, 1894) 1:83.

11. Samuel Austin Allibone, *A Critical Dictionary of English Literature and British and American Authors* (Philadelphia, 1886) 542. In a letter from James Ballantyne to Maria Edgeworth respecting her commendation of *Waverley*, 11 Nov. 1814.

12. "A Postscript Which Should Have Been a Preface," *Waverley* (Boston, 1857) 367-68.

13. "Miss Edgeworth, 1767-1849," *A Book of Sibyls* (London, 1883) 121.

Style and Purpose in Maria Edgeworth's Fiction
by Joanne Altieri

1. © 1968 by the Regents of the University of California. Reprinted from *Nineteenth-Century Fiction*, 23 (1968): 265-67, 272-75, 276-78, by permission of the author and the Regents.

2. *Maria Edgeworth: Chosen Letters*, F. V. Barry, introduction (Boston & New York: 1931) 245. All citations in this paper are to this edition of the letters.

3. See especially chapters 7 and 10 of the *Essay on Irish Bulls*, written with her father, in *Tales and Novels*, 18 vols. (London, 1832) 1.

4. Donald Davie offers an interpretation which disallows the possibility, *The Heyday of Sir Walter Scott* (New York: Barnes, 1961) 65-77. Since I have tried to work consistently outward from style, I have sacrificed the help of previous readings of Maria Edgeworth, of which Davie's is the most thoughtful. In his view her honesty to her moral and social ideas determines both the perfection of the first book and shortcomings of the later ones. This is certainly true: *Castle Rackrent* was fortunate in having no social issue such as absentee landlordism to override its ironies, though its title alone should indicate that social problems are involved. But then, the empirical realism of *Castle Rackrent* has all but vanished from *The Absentee*, where indulgence in conventionalities, moral and stylistic, precludes it. I do not believe, as Davie does, that part of the cause of the change lies in the fact that the social melieu of *Castle Rackrent* is the fading past, the tone it calls up "elegiac." Maria Edgeworth's attitude towards Thady and his masters is far too ironic for any romanticizing of their condition: her satire is aimed at universal follies, regardless of period.

5. It lasted at least through *The Heart of Midlothian*, where the carefully recorded Scots places the "high" speech in strong relief. It is well known that Scott acknowledged his debt to Maria Edgeworth in dialect and interesting that Davie (13) finds his narrative style like *The Absentee's*. I have avoided making comparisons between the two largely

because I do not wish by implication to attach my conclusions to Scott. That would require far more careful study of the latter's work than I have given it.

6. Maria Edgeworth could pick up a convention and use it well. The allegorical naming of Lady Dashfort (cf. Congreve's Wishfort) is an instance of her borrowing well — from the same source.

7. Joseph Wood Krutch in his *Comedy and Conscience after the Restoration* (New York: Columbia U P, 1924) makes a comment apposite to *The Absentee* in his discussion of Steele's comic theory: "In disgust with the dramatic product of the preceding age, Steele threw overboard its whole method, sound as it was, and attempted to found comedy on an impossible principle. The ideally virtuous hero whom he wished to set up must always appear as a perfect monster" (243).

8. *The Gay Couple in Restorian Comedy* (Cambridge, Mass., Harvard U P 1948) 231. Smith's understated comment on the method is that it was one which did not "encourage the production of enduring literature." His location of the radical change in drama around 1700 in the shift from the negative example of satire to the positive example of the sentimental comedy defines precisely the alteration I have tried to show in Maria Edgeworth's novels. That is, the change is one basically of method, not content, though content must be affected.

The Didacticism of Edgeworth's *Castle Rackrent* by Gerry H. Brookes

1. Reprinted from *Studies in English Literature (1500-1900)*, 17 (1977):593-605, with the kind permission of the author and publishers.

2. *Maria Edgeworth's Art of Prose Fiction* (The Hague: Mouton, 1971) 70-71; cited hereafter as Harden. This view can also be found in Emily Lawless, *Maria Edgeworth* (New York: Macmillan, 1904) 87; Roger McHugh, "Maria Edgeworth's Irish Novels," *Studies*, 27 (1938):558; Stephen Gwynn, *Irish Literature and Drama in the English Language: A Short History* (London: Nelson, 1936) 52; P. H. Newby, "The Achievement of Maria Edgeworth," *The Listener*, 41 (1949): 987; W. L. Renwick, *English Literature*, 1789-1815, *The Oxford History of English Literature*, 10 vols. (Oxford, 1963), 8:74.

3. (London: Oxford U P, 1972): 435, 240; cited as Butler.

4. *The Irish Novelists 1800-1850* (New York: Columbia U P, 1959) 68. For similar views see Horatio Sheafe Krans, *Irish Life in Irish Fiction* (New York: Columbia U P, 1903) 29; and Christine Longford, "Maria Edgeworth and Her Circle," *Irish Writing*, 6 (1948; rpt. Nendeln/Liechtenstein: Kraus Reprint, 1970) 73.

5. Still, many critics end up trying to conciliate these two views of the book. Bruce Teets, for example, in his Introduction to *Castle Rackrent* (Coral Gables: U of Florida P, 1964), argues that the book is a "direct transcript from life without any overt theory or moralizing," yet "back of Thady's tale is the implicit moral belief that excess finally leads to disaster" 22, 25-26.

6. I have in mind Sheldon Sacks's definition of an apologue "as a fictional example of the truth of a formulable statement or a series of such statements," *Fiction and the Shape of Belief: A Study of Henry Fielding, With Glances at Swift, Johnson, and Richardson* (Berkeley: U of California P, 1964) 26. This volume will be cited as Sacks. It seems useful to think of apologues as effecting an "attitude" in the reader, which can be represented by a formulation of the "statement" exemplified and a description of the emotions attendant upon that "statement."

7. W. B. Coley says that Maria Edgeworth's "theme is the effect of the past upon the present, particularly as manifested in lingering and ineffective traditions or ingrained cultural habits," "An Early 'Irish' Novelist," *Minor British Novelists*, ed. Charles Alva

Hoyt (Carbondale: U of Illinois, 1967) 22. He argues that the novel is regional but not historical, especially when compared with Scott's novels. [See selection above, Ed].

8. Donald Davie argues that Maria Edgeworth's historical understanding of her characters' situation allows her to sympathize with them, against her rationalist and doctrinal bent, *The Heyday of Sir Walter Scott* (New York: Barnes, 1961) 65-67.

9. Harden and Butler, among others, see Thady as the cause of *Castle Rackrent*, following Maria Edgeworth's hint, mentioned below, about hearing an old steward's voice as she wrote. The insistence that Thady is primary in the tale, that he is represented from the life, and that the tale is less moralistic than her other works, makes it difficult for these critics to see the implications of their indirect perceptions of the didactic intention of this story.

10. Thomas Flanagan says that "it is Thady who creates the illusion of family, out of the feudal retainer's pride in the house which he serves," *The Irish Novelists* 77. This illusion is part of the tension of what Flanagan sees as a plotted novel not as an apologue (see Sacks's first chapter for a discussion of this distinction). Flanagan gives an account of Maria Edgeworth's narrative as "an almost perfect work of fiction," whose purpose "is to bring to life, by plot and symbol, a society which was destroyed by self-deception" 69. Flanagan is right about the purpose of *Castle Rackrent*, but not the means. The powerful plot he describes is not embodied there. [See selections above, Ed.]

11. *Tales and Novels*, The Longford edition, 10 vols. (London, 1893; rpt. Hildesheim: Georg Olms, 1969) 4:85. References to *Irish Bulls* are to this edition.

12. Joanne Altieri discusses the ways in which Thady's speech and state of mind resemble that of the creator of bulls, as described in *Irish Bulls*, "Style and Purpose in Maria Edgeworth's Fiction," *Nineteenth Century Fiction*, 23 (1968-1969):265-278. [See selection above, Ed.]. Although Altieri obscures the idea, implicit in parts of her essay, that the form of *Castle Rackrent* is didactic, much of what she says complements the arguments made here. Ernest A. Baker, in *Edgeworth, Austen, Scott*, vol. 6 of *The History of the English Novel* (London: Witherby, 1929) 30-31, also discusses Thady's bulls. [See selection above, Ed.].

13. *The Rhetoric of Fiction* (Chicago: U of Chicago P, 1961) 70-77.

14. For further discussions of syntax in *Castle Rackrent*, see Joanne Altieri, "Style and Purpose in Maria Edgeworth's Fiction." [See selection above, Ed.].

15. In *Ennui*, Lord Y------, with Maria Edgeworth's obvious sanction, says, "I hold that we are the artificers of our own fortune. If there be any whom the gods wish to destroy, these are first deprived of understanding; whom the gods wish to favour they first endow with integrity, inspire with understanding, and animate with activity," *Tales and Novels* 4:387.

16. Thady seems inconsistent, for example, when he says at one point that he knows nothing of law and later shows considerable knowledge of it (14-16, 40-42). One can see that Maria Edgeworth sacrifices apparent consistency in the latter instance for the purpose of representing the tenuousness of Sir Condy's situation, banking on a prospective inheritance, and of showing, as her footnote tells us, the skill of the Irish poor in law (108-09).

17. Texas Christian U Monographs in History and Culture, No. 2 (Fort Worth, 1967) 144-67. [See selection above, Ed.].

18. See the attack on Newcomer's use of evidence in Harden, 55-56n.

19. This rule is stated in Sacks, 60n.

20. In *Irish Life in Irish Fiction*, Horatio 5. Krans seems to come to such a conclusion. He says that the narrative "is a faithful picture of a national disorder in an acute stage, which, running its course, in a few generations wound up the career of a good part of the old families of the land" 29.

21. See her letter to Mrs Stark of Sept. 6, 1834, in *Maria Edgeworth: Chosen Letters*, ed. F. V.

Barry (Boston: Houghton, 1931) 243.

22. In "A Dozen of Novels," *Frazer's* 9 (1834):483-84, Thackeray works a perverse variation on this argument, reasoning that since working alone after her father's death, she wrote a dull novel, *Helen,* then her father must have written the lively Irish novels.

23. "No. 4," *The Rambler,* ed. W. J. Bate and Albrecht B. Strauss, vol. 3 of *The Yale Edition of the Works of Samuel Johnson* (New Haven & London: Yale U P, 1969) 24-25. Harden shows schematically the kind of balance that Maria Edgeworth gives her examples of virtue and vice in her story, "Waste Not, Want Not," and that she employs with more or less symmetry in most of her fiction, Harden 24-25.

24. This neoclassical balance takes a Utilitarian form in the Edgeworths' thinking. They write: "'The general principle,' that we should associate pleasure with whatever we wish that our pupils should pursue, and pain with whatever we wish they should avoid, forms, our readers will perceive, the basis for our plan of education," *Practical Education,* 2nd ed., 3 vols. (London: 1801) 3:291.

25. Letter to Lady Spencer, May 11, 1803, quoted in Butler, 286-87.

26. In *Children's Books in England: Five Centuries of Social Life,* 2nd ed. (Cambridge: Cambridge U P, 1970), 141-44, F. J. Harvey Darton gives an account of his reading of Maria Edgeworth's "The Purple Jar" that represents accurately the difficulties readers are likely to have with many of her apologues, where she does not succeed in controlling the reader's expectations and desires and subsuming them to her moral purpose, as she does succeed in doing in *Castle Rackrent.*

27. *Lectures on the English Comic Writers,* vol. 6 of *The Complete Works of William Hazlitt,* ed. P. P. Howe, Centenary Edition (London: Dent, 1931) 123.

28. The view of the story presented here is further evidence in support of the idea that Maria Edgeworth offered Sir Walter Scott a formal model for his apologues, as well as models for subject matter and characters, an idea developed by Professor Ralph W. Rader in lectures at the University of California, Berkeley. The idea is also sketched by Donald Davie in *The Heyday of Sir Walter Scott.* The nature of this influence and the nature of the historical apologue, the apologue that exemplifies a view of the past, deserve further study.

ADDITIONAL CRITICISM OF *CASTLE RACKRENT*

Allen, Walter. *The English Novel.* New York: Dutton, 1957. 107-09. A short discussion of Maria Edgeworth's influence on the regional novel.

Buckley, Mary. "Attitudes to Nationality in Four Nineteenth-Century Novelists: 1. Maria Edgeworth." *Journal of the Cork Historical and Archaeological Society* 78 (1973): 27-34. Maria Edgeworth as a critical, though loyal, colonial novelist.

Connelly, Joseph F. "Transparent, Poses: *Castle Rackrent* and *The Memoirs of Barry Lyndon*". *Éire-Ireland* 14 (Samhradh/Summer 1979): 37-43. Despite differences in purpose and scope, these novels exhibit similarities in their Irish dimensions, narrative techniques and humour, suggesting a direct influence.

Cronin, Anthony. *Heritage Now: Irish Literature in the English Language.* New York: St. Martin's, 1982. 17-29. *Castle Rackrent* begins the tradition of Irish literature in English because of its author's interest in national character and its plotless, ambiguous, oral features.

Cronin, John. *The Anglo-Irish Novel. Vol. One. The Nineteenth Century.* Belfast: Appletree, 1980. 25-40. A wide-ranging discussion which concludes that Thady is "a magnificently realised slave, a terrifying vision of the results of colonial misrule."

Davie, Donald. "Maria Edgeworth." *The Heyday of Sir Walter Scott.* London: Routledge &

Kegan Paul, 1961. 65-77. Except for *Castle Rackrent*, which so impressed Scott, the spirit of the Enlightenment pervades Maria Edgeworth's works.

Edwards, Duane. "The Narrator of *Castle Rackrent.*" *South Atlantic Quarterly* 71 (1972):125-29. Contrary to Newcomer's reading (above), Thady is "a sentimental, generally unreflective old man whose love of money causes him to ally himself with Jason, who for some unexplained reason abandons him."

Gwynn, Stephen. *Irish Literature and Drama in the English Language: A Short History.* New York: Nelson, 1936. 48-60. Maria Edgeworth's lack of sympathy for what Thady Quirk "really signified" — Irish nationalist aspirations — accounts for "the amazing detachment" of *Castle Rackrent.*

Harden, Elizabeth. *Maria Edgeworth.* Boston: Twayne, 1984. A fine survey of the life and work with a useful annotated bibliography. This study lays stress on the theme of "the education of the heart" through the various phases of Maria Edgeworth's artistic development.

Henn, T. R. "The Big House." *Last Essays.* New York: Barnes & Noble, 1976. 207-20. A personal and wide-ranging eulogy for the ethos of the gentry of Anglo-Ireland.

Kennedy, Eileen. "Genesis of a Fiction: The Edgeworth-Turgenev Relationship." *English Language Notes* 6 (June 1969): 271-73. Introduces evidence that undermines the often repeated assertion of Turgenev's indebtedness to Maria Edgeworth.

Kilroy, James F. "Maria Edgeworth: Bibliographies, Editions, Biographies, Critical Studies." *Anglo-Irish Literature: A Review of Research.* Ed. Richard J. Finneran. New York: Modern Language Association, 1976. 25-31. A sound bibliographical essay on critical studies of Maria Edgeworth's works. "Maria Edgeworth." *Recent Research on Anglo-Irish Writers.* Ed. Richard J. Finneran. New York: MLA, 1983. 14-15. Supplementary to item above.

Matthews, Brander. Introduction. *Castle Rackrent and The Absentee.* By Maria Edgeworth. London: Dent, 1910. vii-xvii. Briefly outlines the literary and historical contexts for these novels.

McCormack, W. J. *Ascendancy and Tradition in Anglo-Irish Literary History from 1789 to 1939.* Oxford: Clarendon, 1985. 97-122. A wide-ranging discussion of the political circumstances of *Castle Rackrent's* composition, Maria Edgeworth's use of family chronicles, the architecture of the Big House, and issues raised by Butler, Flanagan and Colgan above.

Murray, Patrick. *Maria Edgeworth: A Study of the Novelist.* Cork: Mercier, 1971. 38-40, 50-52. Cursory comments on *Castle Rackrent,* but a cogent discussion of the father-daughter collaboration.

Newby, Percy Howard. *Maria Edgeworth.* Denver: Swallow, 1950. Incisive introduction concluding that "whereas Jane Austen was so much the better novelist Maria Edgeworth may be the more important."

Newcomer, James. *Maria Edgeworth.* Lewisburg: Bucknell UP, 1973. Brief biographical and critical introduction.

Rafroidi, Patrick. *Irish Literature in the Romantic Period (1789-1850),* 2 vols. Gerrard's Cross: Smythe, 1980. Briefly treats Edgeworth as an anti-Romantic (1:5-12), and provides a full bibliography (2:148-56).

Solomon, Stanley J. "Ironic Perspective in Maria Edgeworth's *Castle Rackrent.*" *Journal of Narrative Technique* 2 (1972): 68-73. Thady's unreliability as a narrator implies that his actions are less significant than his omissions.

Teets, Bruce. Introduction. *Maria Edgeworth's Castle Rackrent.* Coral Gables: U. of Miami,

1964. 1-31. A lucid survey of biographical, historical and literary contexts. Considers Thady a naif.

Watson, George. Introduction. *Castle Rackrent*. By Maria Edgeworth. London: Oxford UP, 1964. vii-xxv. Balanced, sophisticated: the best discussion of the novel in print.

Notes on the Essayists

Altieri, Joanne, is an Assistant Professor at the University of Washington, Seattle. Her primary research interest is in literary style, and she has published essays on Carew and Dryden. She is the author of *The Theatre of Praise* (1986), a study of 17th-century English panegyric theatre.

Baker, Ernest (1869-1941), is the author of numerous books in the areas of library management, lexicography, literary history, and the outdoors, especially mountaineering and the Scottish Highlands.

Brookes, Gerry, is an Associate Professor of English at the University of Nebraska-Lincoln, where he teaches writing and Victorian literature. He has published on Carlyle, and has done research in nineteenth-century fiction and non-fictional prose.

Butler, Marilyn, Fellow, Tutor and Lecturer in English at St Hugh's College, Oxford. Besides her biography of Maria Edgeworth, she has published *Jane Austen and the War of Ideas* (1975), *Peacock Displayed: A Satirist and His Context* (1979), and *Romantics, Rebels, and Reactionaries: English Literature and its Background 1760-1830* (1981).

Coley, W. B., is Professor of English at Wesleyan University. He is the executive editor of the Wesleyan Edition of the Works of Henry Fielding, jointly published by Clarendon Press and the Wesleyan University Press. The author of books on Fielding (1974) and Hogarth (1970), from 1969 to 1979 he was associate editor of *College English*.

Colgan, Maurice, is Visiting Lecturer in English, Bradford University, West Yorkshire. He has published essays on the relationships between literature, social conditions, and politics in eighteenth- and nineteenth-century Ireland, including "After Rackrent: Ascendancy Nationalism in Maria Edgeworth's Later Irish Novels," in *Studies in Anglo-Irish Literature*, ed. Heinz Kosok (1982), a sequel to his essay in this collection.

Cronin, John, is Professor of English at the Queen's University, Belfast, having previously lectured at the University of the Witwatersrand, Johannesburg. He is the author of *Somerville and Ross* (1972), *Gerald Griffin 1803-1840: A Critical Biography* (1978) and *The Anglo-Irish Novel: Vol. 1, The Nineteenth Century* (1980). He is a member of the Committee for the Study of Anglo-Irish Literature at the Royal Irish Academy.

Flanagan, Thomas, since 1978 has been Professor at the State University, of New York at Stonybrook. He previously taught at Columbia, The University of California at Los Angeles and Berkeley. Besides his criticism, he has published short stories and novels, including *The Year of the French* (1979).

Harden, Elizabeth, is Professor of English at Wright State University, Dayton, Ohio. Her major research interests are Anglo-Irish literature, the English Romantic poets, and the nineteenth-century British novel. She has studied in Ireland and England and is the author of *Maria Edgeworth* (Boston: Twayne, 1984).

Ó hÓgáin, Dáithí, lectures in Irish Folklore at University College, Dublin. He has published several books on folk and literary topics, and is also an accomplished poet and short story writer in Irish. His best-known academic works are *An File* (1982), a study of the image of the poet in Irish tradition, and *The Hero in Irish Folk History* (1985).

McHugh, Roger (1908-87), was the first Professor of Anglo-Irish literature drama at University College, Dublin. His plays, *Trial at Green Street Courthouse* (1941) and *Rossa* (1945) were produced at the Abbey Theatre. He has written or edited numerous works in Irish history and literature, including collections of letters from Yeats to Katherine Tynan (1953) and Margot Ruddock (1970), most recently, with Maurice Harmon, *A Short History of Anglo-Irish Literature* (1982).

Newcomer, James, Vice-Chancellor Emeritus, Texas Christian University, former Trustees Professor of English and Director of TCU Press. Besides his work on Maria Edgeworth, he has published *Celebration* (poems, 1973), *The History of Luxembourg: The Evolution of Nationhood* (1984), *The Resonance of Grace* (poems, 1984), and *Lady Morgan: The Novelist* (forthcoming).

Owens, Cóilín, is Associate Professor of English, George Mason University. A native of Ireland, educated there and in the United States, he has taught in Japan and at various American institutions. He has published numerous articles and reviews on Joyce and in the field of Irish studies.